I WILL BE

Faithful

I WILL BE

Faithful

ELLIE WOLF

BATTLE GROUND
creative

Published in Houston, Texas, by Battle Ground Creative
First Edition

ISBN softcover: 978-1-947554-98-6
RELIGION / Christian Living / Personal Memoirs

Battle Ground Creative is a publishing company with an emphasis on helping first-time authors find their voice. Named after an obscure city in Washington State, we currently operate offices in Houston, Texas and Philadelphia, Pennsylvania. For a complete title list and bulk order information, please visit www.battlegroundcreative.com

Unless otherwise indicated, Scriptures are taken from the NEW AMERICAN STANDARD BIBLE®, Copyright © 1960, 1962, 1963, 1968, 1971, 1972, 1973, 1975, 1977, 1995 by The Lockman Foundation. Used by permission.

Scriptures marked NIV taken from THE HOLY BIBLE, NEW INTERNATIONAL VERSION®, NIV® Copyright © 1973, 1978, 1984, 2011 by Biblica, Inc.™ Used by Permission. All rights reserved worldwide.

Edited by Jared Stump
Cover design by Christina Zhang
Cover photo by Samara Doole (Unsplash.com)
Interior design and typeset by Katherine Lloyd

Printed in the United States of America

Cassie,
Thank you for your support of what's now in your hands! Hope all's well.

This book is for those who have
suffered immeasurable pain in their lives.
There is always hope and healing in Christ.

Ellie
30 Nov 20

CONTENTS

ACKNOWLEDGEMENTS

*M*y thanks go out to my mother, sisters, and brothers. Mom has always been a constant support to encourage me to do fun, crazy things she couldn't see herself doing (her words). My siblings have encouraged me in this writing process, as well as in the way of championing one another to grow up into decent adults, despite adversity we have shared and experienced individually. And to all the friends and coffee shops that hosted me while I wrote, as well as my friends who participated in the Indiegogo fundraiser and donated through other means: Thank you everyone for helping make this possible.

Names of all donors: Melissa, Kenneth, Brooke, Carolyn, Bryce, Mark and Sara, Melissa, Laura, Amy, Leah, Jake and Marlana, William, Neil and Debbie, Greg, Clare, Mark and Eileen, John, David, Frank and Lynn, Cassie, Lindsay and Janet, Nicole, Brenda, Ashley, Elizabeth, Jill, Blair, Alex and Sarah, Andrew, Joseph and Brenna, Mike and Sara, Greg and Lisa, Armin and Megan, Jim and Andrea.

AUTHOR'S NOTE

*I*t required a lot of prayer and reliance on the Lord to arrive at a place of healing where I could feel comfortable opening up about the struggles I had growing up—especially since I am writing about them for all to read. Arriving at this place took a great deal of time and courage. My hope is that this book will bring glory to God and show His marvelous healing power is still at work even today.

Parents and those sensitive to disturbing content should be forewarned when reading. I do delve into the details and the unfortunate realities of depression and rape. This book is very transparent, it does show glimpses of my journey through struggles with trauma and grief.

As a memoir, some names have been changed or withheld altogether; others are used with permission from the individuals. This content is my perception of events, at the time of submission to the publisher.

Blessed are those whose help is the God of Jacob,
    whose hope is in the Lord their God.

He is the Maker of heaven and earth,
    the sea, and everything in them—
    he remains faithful forever.

He upholds the cause of the oppressed
    and gives food to the hungry.
The Lord sets prisoners free,
    the Lord gives sight to the blind,
    the Lord lifts up those who are bowed down,
    the Lord loves the righteous.
The Lord watches over the foreigner
    and sustains the fatherless and the widow,
    but he frustrates the ways of the wicked.

~ Psalm 146:5-9, NIV

Chapter 1

DADDY'S GIRL

ineteen years ago, my world came to a screeching halt.

With tears continually running down her cheeks, like a river, and grief paralyzing each sound that squeaked through her voice, my mother explained what had just happened. It was blunt, quick, and news that no child should ever have to hear.

"Your dad just died … in a car accident. One day, a long time from now, you'll see him again in Heaven. But he is gone."

I remember that conversation like it was yesterday and where we all were. My little brother sitting on my mom's lap up on the couch, my little sister snuggled closely next to him, and my big sister and me on the floor together. We all looked at her completely dumbfounded as she spoke, blank stares on our faces, trying to absorb the news as small children. On a typical day, we might be sitting in these places listening to my mom read aloud *The Chronicles of Narnia* or Laura Ingalls Wilder books. However, this day was anything but typical.

Earlier that day, my dad had been driving to an appointment. While on his way, not far from our home, there was a power outage across a major intersection, due to construction. All three of the drivers involved in the crash attempted to pass through at the same time. Brakes were slammed and steering wheels were cranked, but these actions were not enough to save everybody. His Subaru was t-boned by an SUV that sent him smashing into a second SUV. He was soon retrieved by paramedics and rushed to the hospital. Although he had worn his seatbelt, it was no match for the massive impact that occurred.

That was the morning of Tuesday, April 14, 1998. That day I lost my hero and my mom was left to raise four young children all on her own.

My family members all have slightly different recollections of what happened that day. From my remembrance, once Mom got the call, she dashed out of her lesson plans, pulled each of us out of our classes, raced home, went with a friend to identify his body while another friend stayed with us, came home, and sat everyone down. At that moment, all us kids knew was that "there was an accident" but nothing more.

I remember missing ballet class that afternoon. It was a few hours after we got home and our mom was not back yet.

I went to the lady watching us and told her, "Guess what? My ballet class starts soon." She started looking for her keys, offering to load up the car and take me to my class if I could get ready quickly.

I said, "No, it is okay to miss sometimes… and I prefer to be here whenever Mommy comes back." We skipped that class.

According to my mom's memory, we came home after Bible Study with no knowledge of the accident, and she saw the message light on the phone blinking quickly. She listened to the message which turned out to be a friend asking to call her right then, as soon as we got home. The friend told her over the phone that my dad had been in an accident. She would take Mom to the hospital while another friend would stay with us kids. We were given a few chores to do while they were gone. At that point, she did not know he was already passed.

Once they came home from the hospital, Mom said she would prefer to, "tell the kids on her own." We still had no idea what was going on. She said that the two ladies could leave, phone the congregation, and come back later. Mom sent me to promptly bring a box of tissues to the living room because she had to tell us "something life-changing." And with that news, my childhood world, up to that point, was over.

———

I pray that no child will ever have to go through what happened next. Standing in front of your daddy's coffin at the wake, your seven-year-old hand on his frigid and lifeless 43-year-old arm, trying everything you know to help him "wake up" and play with you again, all the while knowing he will never wake up. The longer I stood there trying to revive him, the more I was told by adults "he is really gone forever," the more I grasped the concept of death. This is when I lost my childlike hope for miracles.

After the wake, we filed into the limo which took us to and from the church for the service. I asked my mom why the seating arrangement is across instead of the wide-open limos in movies. At first the expression on her face appreciated the ignorance of my question, but quickly changed as she tried to maintain composure and make it to through the next moment.

We waited in the holding room for it to be time to go into the sanctuary to hear my dad's friends and business partners all share dear and funny stories, one after another. Amidst countless outdoor adventure stories, everyone had something to share about their favorite pranks and jokes my dad regularly performed. I was placed in between one of my aunts and my big sister Laine, wondering how they could cry the whole hour and a half, but my tear ducts seemed to be as frozen as ice caps. My heart was lollygagging, as a seven-year-old's ought to. Soon, the frozen tundra in my eyes melted like a snow-covered mountain in the springtime. The nights following my best friend's death, my pillow was soaked with my tears after being tucked in by only Mom or babysitters. I missed him deeply.

The foot traffic in and out of our house was untamable the next six months, fading slowly. During this time, we were so blessed with help from people. Droves of volunteers came to our house as babysitters, cooks, and even friends taking care of odd jobs around the house. Especially throughout the years of 1998 and 1999, while we were still homeschooled, there was always someone extra we knew and were comfortable with at our house. At times, we had friends take us to their house to give Mom some respite. For the next three Christmases, people from different churches came by with cars packed to the roofs of gifts for our family. Of the generosity shown from these strangers, I still use one of the gifts each of us girls received which was an angel pendant. Despite the wear and tear from the years, I still wear it on a chain along with a little ring with the word "hope" on it, which I once found in an old box of junk. Between physical gifts and people volunteering their time and talents, we were undoubtedly blessed beyond words for many years.

I was in the second grade when my dad passed. My third-grade year was just a blank void, academically, as far as my memory is concerned. Laine reminded me that this year our family faced recurring basement flooding and medical stresses, between trips to visit our mom's family on the west coast. It is probably for the best that I cannot remember. I'm sure that life was not so easy that year.

Fourth grade came and the transition from homeschooling to public school was a tough one for me. I was at a third-grade level for math, writing, and reading. Homeschoolers often spread a couple of grades in their workbooks at a time, according to ability, and had less of a structured day. Once your schoolwork was completed, you were free to play. Being in different grade levels for certain subjects was not as weird to me as it may have been for my classmates.

The next school year, fifth grade, was rough on a whole new level. I remember that on the anniversary of my dad's accident, I approached each of my classmates during the lunch hour and asked around if anyone would be willing "to help me die early." I just missed my dad so much every day. I was tired of being "a strong little girl," and helping my mom so much at home. I did not see this as a suicidal mentality; I simply wanted to be with him again. I wanted him to help me understand math. I wanted him to scoop me up and lift me onto his shoulders and run around singing together. I wanted to see him look at my mom with that subtle assurance he consistently carried that said, "Hey, I love you and everything will somehow always be all right because we have the Lord leading us." I was tired of the dreams that I woke up from with tears, where he came around corners of familiar places and picked me up and swung me around like he used to. I was emotionally finished with those dreams; I just wanted *him*. I understood that in order to "see" him again, I had to be in Heaven so that is where I was determined to be. Thankfully, at least two friends went to the class aide who came to me and pulled me aside.

"Ellie, a couple of the students just came to me saying you are looking for help to end your life. Why is that?" I explained my little ten-year-old philosophy and her eyes became misty. She went to get the teachers from the staff lounge that brought the principals into the matter. The principal called my mom. The teacher, assistant principal, principal, and I had a little pow-wow in the office that day which ended with, "Any time you feel this desire, just let your teachers know and you can come hang out here with us for a little bit before going back to class." I will admit to you that I did shamelessly abuse this offer from time to time. For example, if there was a quiz I didn't know enough answers on I would ask to be excused for the class period.

Throughout the years following my dad's death, our family saw consistent financial provision. My mom did not have to immediately put us in childcare or have to work fulltime. When she did have to find a job, the hours were flexible with getting each of us to and from school. She worked as an aide for a local state official. God always saw that we were taken care of and money was not a dire stress. My mom is generous while very good at saving money and only spending when necessary. From the time of the accident, as long as she was in charge of the finances, everything always worked out. We all grew up with an understanding of the difference between needs and wants. Money doesn't grow on trees or fall from the sky; however, when it looked like there wasn't enough, God somehow always took care of any difference or lack.

I can only remember a few things about my dad.

My dad was a tall and thin man, upright in many ways. He was a solid pillar of faith, respectable, and always present for his family. He was steady and intelligent. He knew what it meant to love and be loved.

As an adult, I know that the aching and missing him doesn't ever completely stop; the yearning for his hugs, laughter, or presence is never fulfilled. But it is also no longer a constant obsession. Grief, from my experience, comes in unexpected waves, typically in the still, calm moments that I remember sharing similar, sweet times with him. When the waves hit, what best consoles me is human contact. We all need supportive relationships, and it may be extra important to those who are going through grief. We were not designed to be alone all the time. We each need to give and receive support and healthy physical touch from time to time in order to continue developing.

The sadness hits at very random times, often taking even me off guard. It's very common for me to be sitting in a crowd of my friends with a complete blank stare on my face, one that is void of all expression. Many times, my friends will ask me if I'm okay and what I'm thinking. It puzzles me at first as I rarely realize it is happening again, but after a few moments I realize *why* those questions are relevant and it comes back to this:

I still miss my dad, *terribly.*

My mother has explained grief in a way that I think makes perfect sense. She always says, "For many, the 'waves' of it come and go forever, in and out like the tide. You can find a new normal and seem to be progressing toward a healthy and healed place, and then something happens and throws you backwards."

Ten years after losing my dad, I was talking with a friend about my loss. He told me that I should have been over this whole "losing my dad thing" and that it had "been long enough to process, mourn, and move on." This was a common response from many of my peers. It's not really their fault; those who haven't experienced such a trauma or loss can't comprehend the cycle of grief in such depth, so you have to simply forgive what they can never understand.

I wish that no child ever dreams of running into their daddy around town and getting a big hug before waking up and crying because it was just a dream. That dream was always my favorite because normally he would spin me around like he would when we went to the park. He would take my arms and we spun for what feels like hours but, in reality, was only a few moments. In my dreams, I always saw him smile and sometimes heard his voice. Now, years have passed since I have seen or heard either. I would give nearly anything to begin having these dreams again. I would give anything to have him back.

I believe the experiences a child has when they are little are particularly impactful. To this day, flowers still take me back to his funeral. The smell and association is so entrenched in my brain that I go back to that place so many years later. I adore the beauty and creativity expressed through creation, but smelling flowers still hurts my heart. Little by little, I'm less bothered by them. There are now times I can smell flowers without my thoughts shifting toward death, loss, and pain. Healing comes, but not without a lot of time, distance, and a willingness to heal. We all learn our "new normal."

Chapter 2

OUR NEW NORMAL

*F*our years after my dad's fatal accident, my mom met someone new. She was introduced to him by a mutual friend and they hit it off. The first time Mom took us to meet him, he hosted the five of us for dinner in his little ranch-hand house where he lived working for the rancher. Even though I'd only visited a handful of times, I still remember the floor plan vividly. First, enter into the living room which is open to the small dining room and an equally small kitchen. To the right, was his bedroom and to the left, were the bathroom and a second bedroom. This bedroom was decorated for a young boy.

"Do you have any kids?" we asked, not yet knowing much about him. He explained that he did have one son from his previous marriage.

"Is he playing with the rancher's kids right now?" We

figured if we were to meet our mother's boyfriend and see his house that we would certainly get to meet his son.

"Not today," he laughed. "My son lives with his mom back in Florida, where I am from. You'll meet him next time he comes to visit."

We heard the *ding* of the kitchen timer. The new boyfriend and Mom went to fix the spaghetti and French bread. We all ran into the bathroom to wash our hands and enjoyed our dinner as a group. Sometimes they had dates out, at his little place, or movie nights with us at our house. To me, it felt like Mom did a lot of driving either way because his car was rarely reliable.

The second time I remember us all being together was about a month later, near Mother's Day. Mom's boyfriend invited us down to the ranch to ride one of the horses. He helped us up and then led on foot. We seemed to have a good time, things seemed to be progressing well and fairly normal. While we were there, my little sister Josie started feeling sick as she had unknowingly contracted the chickenpox from a friend at school that week. In an effort to make her feel better, not knowing she would soon break out in spots, I sat outside on the barn porch with her and rubbed her back as she held back the feeling to vomit. Not too long after her chickenpox, I got them, for the second time in my childhood.

Later in the summer, we were at the ranch for a big horse-cutting event, a shindig that ranchers put on to show off their horses and wrangling skills, a mini rodeo of sorts. Watching people roping horses is only fun for a twelve-year-old city girl to watch for so long. After a couple hours, I asked my mom if my little sister, brother, and I could venture over to the fishing pond, which was just across the way from the barn. Before she could say "Yes, if you are careful not to fall in" her boyfriend jumped up and said he would walk us over. I assured them that I knew how to get there, but he insisted.

I remember there was a strange tension, so I tried to walk to the pond quickly so he would leave. This did not work so well because he gently pulled me back and started making small talk. I began to realize he was trying to spend some time with me and I wasn't sure why. The water was within sight and I knew if I could hem and haw just a little bit, the chit chat may not last too long. I normally did not mind talking with adults, as there were many trusted family friends who pitched in after Dad's accident, but something was different this day.

He stopped walking and we made eye contact for a moment.

"I have to tell you something," he began before I broke away and headed for the water. He called me back and started over, maintaining eye contact this time.

"Your mom and I are talking about getting married," he uttered firmly.

Looking back, fifteen years later, I can still recount how my little heart felt like it stopped for a split second then started to beat with what felt like three times its normal pace as my hands began to get sweaty. I wanted to yell, "*NO, ABSOLUTELY NOT!*" and run past the pond, up the mile-long driveway, perhaps all the way home. All I knew, and all I wanted, was my family of five. I wanted us to live in our home, the way it was, without him. Besides, we barely knew him. Why did he think he was good enough to be part of our family?

25

Instead, being the "people pleaser" personality that I was, swallowed my doubts, looked back at him and said, "Umm, I guess that is okay with me. Is that all you wanted to talk about?"

He responded with a nod.

"Great! I'm going to go play now. Bye."

After all, what we knew of him at this point was agreeable. He proclaimed faith in the Lord, told us he attended an evangelical church, offered to attend premarital counseling with mom at our church where he got the green light from the pastor.

What we knew about him seemed good. He was charming and charismatic, had one son who would become our new youngest brother. My siblings and I enjoyed his pasta dinners and being at the ranch with the horses. Our dog even liked him. There was nothing that gave anyone pause as to why he and Mom shouldn't move forward with marriage. However, the lingering feeling in the pit of my stomach told me something wasn't quite right, and I regretted voicing my approval from the moment those words left my lips near the pond. It felt as though they were moving too fast, but who was I to say "no" to a chance my mom could be happy?

No more than an hour later, I watched from under the bleachers as he playfully led her out a side door. As he did, he pulled a ring from his pocket, they kissed, and began making their way back into the crowd. It felt like a scene from a movie and she looked so happy—almost as happy as I remember her being before the accident. She was simply beaming.

I went from there to where my older sister, Laine, was sitting on the porch, passing the time with a book in her hand. I told her about the walk to the pond then about what just happened out the side door.

"Yeah, I knew they were going to get engaged today," she said, nonchalantly.

WHAT?! How could she not warn me beforehand? If I knew this was coming I would not have been too flabbergasted to respond and would have a respectful, "this is too soon" response ready when he approached me for "my permission."

My sister continued on, in her infinite 14-year-old wisdom, explaining, "Mom will do whatever she wants. What we think or want really doesn't make a difference. She thinks about us, of course, but she's lonely, too."

Growing up, Mom had always encouraged us to have long engagements. Later on, based on this experience, she added that we shouldn't marry a divorcé—namely one with large responsibilities like child support. (Of course, every situation is different and some men rock the "single dad" lifestyle.) The first weekend of my seventh-grade year, we witnessed her do the exact opposite. We stood alongside them as they married at the home of the friend who introduced them. They had made it through premarital counseling with flying colors and now, eight months after meeting, they were tying the knot.

The wedding itself was memorable mostly because the friend who hosted it only does memorable events. Aside from the décor, I remember it all as if it were yesterday. Meeting our step-family, how odd it felt being one of my own mom's three bridesmaids, how our stepbrother was not present because his mom decided to take him to visit her family up north, how adorable my own baby brother was in a suit, all of us dressed up in our best and jumping on the trampoline with the hosts' kids, the toasts my mom's brother and friend made, the wedding cake enjoyed poolside, being driven home in a party limousine that was a surprise for the newlyweds who didn't want it, opting instead to use it to send us kids home at bedtime.

Being that they were both political junkies, they honeymooned for a week in Washington, D.C. and their marriage was great—for a grand total of three months. He moved into our home and we were beginning to settle into the new dynamics of going from a family of five to a family of seven. We could already tell it wasn't everything they promised it would be, and we quickly picked up on the atmosphere shift that took place in our home.

Everything had to be brand-new for the two newest members of the family. Secondhand finds were outrageously offensive. For example, the annual "back to school shopping" seasons of those first couple of years of transition were always intense. Due to his awful credit rating, our stepdad had to pay in cash, which always came from Mom.

He would head to the door and call out to our stepbrother, "Son, put your shoes on. We are going school shopping."

"Can we go to McDonald's while we're out, too?!" our stepbrother would reply. He nearly always got what he wanted, while the rest of us stayed home to enjoy whatever Mom fixed for dinners.

The majority of the time, our stepdad worked inconsistent jobs from home, mostly freelance sports writing. Since he was home, he always found a way to interject himself in any sibling disagreements we had. If there was arguing or fighting, we had a very short moment to defend our side of the matter before being sent to our rooms or grounded. In any argument that involved our stepbrother, he always ruled in favor of his son. He had a loud, booming voice and was not afraid of using it. But it wasn't only sibling disagreements that got him all worked up. He was very emotional and irrational when it came to sports teams, specifically when the Chicago Bears. We all knew the fastest way out of the house at the end of a game if it wasn't looking good. If his team lost, he immediately went on a rampage of cursing, stomping around, slamming doors, and breaking things. He was often be angry for hours. We knew we were in the clear if he decided to skip dinner and go on a fast food run that night. We lived in a constant state of walking on eggshells when it came to his moods.

As a result of observing my stepdad's erratic behavior while growing up, few things in life trigger me quite like coarse yelling. I simply cannot stand it! Throughout our grade school years, even when he was not angry, we could hear our stepdad's deep voice reverberating from the bedroom as he talked to Mom. Still, he would yell and throw things on a daily basis. Harsh tones and slamming doors were his most common methods to create silence before he moved to the couch in a huff for a few days. It was these unsettling nights that I would find myself on the floor of my closet, doors closed as barriers, listening to my MP3 player as loud as possible in an attempt to drown it all out. Yet, even though I would close my door and hide, I never felt completely safe. Sometimes, we would come home from school and Mom would tell us he was gone at a hotel again and no one knew when he would be back.

Mom was not the only one who would be yelled at on a regular basis. We were all frequently targeted or caught in crossfire—some of us more than others—depending on his mood. Objects would be thrown across the room, and when he would slam doors I would stand facing them, amazed that they hadn't cracked from the force. On more than one occasion, I remember being yelled at for playing the piano while he was trying to work or nap at odd times. There was no winning. We always felt like we were walking a tightrope, trying desperately not to look down. I lived with a great deal of fear and anxiety through these years, and still find that I stutter a bit every now and then as a result.

For some reason, I seemed to be singled out for mistreatment from my stepdad more than the other kids were. After school, my older sister either had work or said, "Hi, we're home!" and then quickly went up to her room to read, study, or listen to music. We wouldn't see her until dinner, and she never got in trouble. When I reached her age, I followed suit and began to hide in my room after school. However, it seemed that every time I would shut my door, his voice boomed, "Hey! … *GET BACK DOWN HERE.* Why are you always trying to be in your room whenever you are home? Come be with the family!"

This would often happen even when the rest of the family was scattered throughout the house doing their own things. If I had homework, I would often have to move my related belongings and do it in his presence. Other times, I would try and sneak out whichever door was the closest just to get away before he knew I was there. If I acted like I didn't hear his voice, depending on his mood, he would just yell all the louder or stomp up the stairs and confront me face to face.

Even at meal times I would almost always end up stuck sitting next to him at the table, attempting to avoid direct eye contact. When it was my turn to set the table, I would always do my best to make sure my place setting was a few seats away from him. I guess my other siblings felt the same way, because I would often see that my spot had been rearranged at the last second, thus forcing me into the "hot seat" right next to him, which of course meant even more belittling and sarcasm. There was no winning or escaping him. Needless to say, I always cleared my plate super-fast and asked to be excused as quickly as possible.

It eventually came to the point where if I heard his footsteps and saw his shadow coming toward my room, I would shudder, panic, and try to hide. My heart would pound so furiously in my chest that I felt it might break loose. I felt so fearful and anxious. As his steps passed my room, I would feel both my heart and my breath stop altogether as I'd pretend to be invisible, until his next few steps faded off down the hallway. On the occasions when he decided to pause and knock—or just tear the door open—I'd quickly answer most of his questions or reply, "I don't know, please leave." He usually left my room with a firm slam of the door. It was as if he felt the need to declare his dominance as often as possible.

As my high school years progressed, I started to grow nervous that he would become physically violent. Thankfully, this did not occur, as far as I can remember. Nonetheless, night after night I hid further and further beneath my bedding, or deeper in the closest, encased in fear. I truly hated him. As I grew older into my adolescence, he'd belittle me all the more and claim I was just a "hormonal girl" any time I tried to speak up about mistreatment. He either simply did not care or was fully blind to the way he treated our family and never saw or owned the cause and effect of his own actions.

I had been homeschooled for many years and later transitioned to small public or private schools. The way my small high school did graduations was a little different from most. There is a portion during the presentation of diplomas when a brief recording from each of the graduates' parents plays as they come to the stage and the principal presents the student with their diploma. A photographer then takes a quick photo, and the student presents a rose to their mother while their father is on stage, close behind. For obvious reasons, I did not want my stepdad involved in this ensemble. The last place he needed to be was on stage with my mother and I, potentially crying and hugging, appearing to the world like he was a caring guy who supported my academia. A big deal was made about him not being included in this graduation rehearsal ordeal and it was addressed by my mom (who did the recording on her own) on the ride home from the rehearsal evening. In the end, I conceded that he could attend my graduation but was not permitted at any of my future life events, specifically my wedding.

The summer and autumn following high school graduation, I was trying to recover from my depression, which I'll discuss in the next chapter. In the summer and fall, I was working three jobs in order to stay distracted and out of the house and to avoid my stepdad as much as possible. I held many roles, which included barista, retail associate, and children's theater assistant director. It wasn't long before I learned that simply being busy wasn't enough to cover the emotional scars of the prior ten years. I developed an eating disorder around the same time. For months, I lived on water and ten saltine crackers each day, with a Luna Bar thrown in every few days for a little variety. This anorexic behavior really was a manifestation of control. I could not control my stepdad, home life, or family, but I *could* control my eating. Balancing three jobs only lasted a few months because I realized it was entirely too much to manage. I later met some good friends through theater and at a local Christian university. These friends did their best at keeping me accountable and helping me get well. Many times, appealing to my sarcastic coping mechanism of a shell, they would sarcastically say, "Would you like some plate with that food there?" or genuinely "Here, take this too ..." against my protest. It was their tough love and my growing maturity that started to ease me "out of myself" and the world I had created to barely survive.

Over time, I realized that verbal abuse is a widespread issue. I began to see it in one of my jobs as a babysitter. It didn't take too long for me to realize there was some major dysfunction in this particular family. The family members would be yelling one moment, crying in another, and hugging after that. It was a constant state of instability with no sense of balance or consistency. It began to remind me of life in my home with my stepdad. When I would babysit for them, I would try to teach the kids that they didn't have to yell and punch things, or me, to get their way or be seen, hoping it would make a difference. One day, the kids asked me what I was reading when they saw me with my Bible open. They asked more questions once I introduced them to Jesus Christ and explained that the cross hanging up in their kitchen was a reminder of what He had done out of love for each person in the whole world. I also explained a little about how there is an enemy who tries to divide people with hate and hurt. They considered these things and then decided to try and stay united and love each other, even when they don't get their way. These lessons on grace and forgiveness were important for them to learn.

Another occurrence where I saw aftermath of such pain and abuse was in one of my friend's homes where he formerly yelled harshly at his family daily. One afternoon, he yelled at his younger teenage brother so harshly that the brother stuttered whenever he spoke for nearly four months. He was later freed from this habit, after Jesus reintroduced Himself to the older brother who reconciled the brotherhood. The whole family has seen awesome restoration and today they continue to pursue a lifestyle that honors God, starting with their words.

You'll never know when God will open up doors to help those who have been hurt like you have. One of my best memories on this comes from a trip across Texas while traveling with a fundraising team during my time with Youth With A Mission (YWAM). The team had decided to stop at McDonald's for a quick break. As I approached the counter, I casually asked the cashier, "Hey, how's it going?" He was shocked by this. The following five minutes he talked about how nobody ever asks him how he's doing; they just come in and start ordering.

I said, "That's silly, you are a person too and just as valuable as the patrons."

This word about *value* took us into a twenty-minute conversation while he tidied the lobby. My road trip team kindly waited in the van. What happened next was amazing. While cleaning tables, this young man proceeded to admit to me that his dad beats him, verbally belittles him, and treats him in ways no father should ever treat their child. Through this divine appointment, I was given the opportunity to share God's love for him, breaking curses and lies that rested on him. I did my best to speak the truth about how loved he is and shared the Gospel, in a McDonald's in a tiny east Texas town.

Verbal abuse leaves emotional scars and is demeaning. Yelling communicates to the victim, *It is possible that I am wrong, but I am still better than you. You don't know what you are talking about. You are wrong. You are stupid, and you clearly do not know anything.*

I love this quote from L.R. Knost: "Yelling silences your message. Speak quietly so children can hear your words instead of just your voice."

I have noticed when people yell at each other it creates extra tension between them as they talk down to each other. Or, in a one-way scenario, the abused eventually shuts down emotionally (and, sometimes, physically) as they fight to maintain self-preservation. The abuser takes this as a victory, knowingly or not, and continues on their tirade.

I was taught in a workshop from Loom International that it takes ten positive affirmations to undo one negative word spoken over someone. It's amazing the amount of damage that can occur from something so simple as our words. The way we talk and the tone in which we communicate can either be a positive or negative force; it's up to us to make that choice.

I selfishly begged my mom for years to divorce my step-dad, never knowing the full extent of how he treated anyone besides me. I was uncomfortable and tried so hard to speak out against unjust situations, but she had her reasons to try to make the marriage work for as long as possible.

All these years later, I fully try to forgive my stepdad for his actions, and every time he projected his own insecurities onto me. In my heart, I have released him and his behaviors. I pray for him and his son, and I hope their relationship will flourish in a healthy way. I especially hope that he has felt the pure, redemptive, presence of God.

God is a father, and He is good. A term recently introduced at my church is *spiritual parents.* The Holy Spirit stays in place of a mentor, as nobody can do what He does, but then parents are the next to exemplify the Lord. My own biological parents did this beautifully until we lost my dad. Afterward, my mom tried to do her best. Later on, God provided me with heavenly "adopted" parents along the way. They are solid and upright people of faith. Having this "adopted" set of parents does not mean that I have left my actual family. However, their example in how they led their family was healing and influential to me. That is actually the best part, watching *how* they led. Their kids have introduced me to new friends as an "adopted big sister," which I absolutely love. In turn, this has given me a place to encourage them in their own lives, and to be the person I needed when I was their ages as God has helped heal me through the parent's examples.

Since my dad's accident, God has delivered and fulfilled me in every way an earthly father should. He approves of me, loves me dearly, and is my Provider. As a child, I never saw severe lack or poverty in our home. In fundraising for multiple trips, I saw Him pay my way and the ways of others creatively through family, friends, strangers, and scholarships at the last minute before deadlines, more than once. It is funny, and nerve wracking, when money shows up out of the blue, like a high five from God saying "Hey, watch how I do it *this* time!" He has never abandoned me or let me go hungry. The Lord always guides me when invited to yet allows me make my own choices. He is good and gentle. But most of all … He is faithful.

Chapter 3

THE ANGELS CRIED

Shadows of the Past
Advanced Writing
Ellie Wolf, Grade 10

She was second oldest out of three children, often over-looked. She had her "feeling left out" moments much more frequently than the "in on everything" ones. She regularly sat in her room, dark and alone.

The only other person she talked with at times like these was someone via texting. This friend tried every-thing he could to keep her spirits up; he was her optimistic pill. Despite his help, she continued feeling empty, lost, and afraid. Holding back tears was her pastime; being fake was the normal routine.

They were both sophomores at the same school, trying to make it through graduation. Day by day, his life seemed to advance—getting better and better with every breath, while her life crumbled every time she did; the past was burned onto her brain and heart, never to leave her alone.

When she was a young girl, she lost someone extremely important and special to not just her, but the whole family: close, extended, and people they classified as family because they were so tight. This man left the world by means of screeching tires, smashing glass, and skid marks. Because of this incident, she felt like the world turned its back on her.

School was a hinder to her life, feeling like she was being held back, she did not try very hard to excel. Like any parent in this situation, hers became especially upset with her.

The more time passed, life appeared as a big blur. Friends entered and departed. She drifted from her parents. Images flashed through her mind every second. Images of how she might die—of what would happen to all the people she befriended during the heart-rending life she led. She always pictured what it would have felt like if she were with her father on the fatal day he was taken by angels. Would she have lived, or die the same death of the driver?

Flashbacks to that day occur every couple of minutes. The smells, tastes, pictures, and activities of the day are embedded on her mind, forever. The aroma of the day was simply "air," not sugar coated nor misty. Any food was simplistic, possibly bland. Pictures were of large churches, flowers, numerous cars, traffic signals and lights. On this day, she went with her mother, brother and sisters to a church where her mom had a meeting; the children went into another room and did their schoolwork. That night, she missed dance class, but held herself together for Awanas, then Bible study the next morning. "Movies" constantly play over and over on the "DVD" player in her long-term memory ...

Contemplating whether to hold on for something or just let go had been the recent issue for this teen girl. Options constantly ran through her mind's eye like a marathon runner: the ways she could go. The possibilities seemed endless, but her three selected favorites, if you will, included rope in the basement, knife in the closet, or set off on a joy ride. If it were up to her, it would still exist as a debate.

Often times when confiding in some friends, she related life to a deck of cards, all neat and tidy until the card owner decides to play fifty-two card pick up. Another analogy was the end of a computer solitaire game, life is currently messed up—like how the cards get crazy at the end of each winning game.

Most girls love the smell of flowers, every girl except her. Whenever she smells any type, it triggers the motion picture of the horrific day of her seven-year-old life. Smelling flowers make her stomach flip, turn, and twist in all different directions at once. If she never smelled another flower in her life, she would be grateful.

This shy girl, timid and scared by almost anything, tried to live life as if nobody watched. Life was to be lived like a secret scandal: happening, but not spoken. One of her favorite quotes comes from her favorite movie, A Walk to Remember: "Love is like the wind: you can't see it, but you know it is there." Her school friend tried many-a-time to remind her of this. Every time they talked he reminded her of all the people who loved her and asked what would happen to them if she left the face of the planet. Pity she was too foolish and stubborn not to heed his words.

This was a piece I wrote and turned in for an assignment during my sophomore year of high school, shortly after depression took ahold of me. As a result, my teachers began to send more and more letters home to my mom, most of which I intercepted.

Looking back, I could have been way less obvious if I didn't secretly want to be helped.

⁓

I naively thought I had battled my depression and had overcome victoriously during my earlier school years. I was so wrong. My depression was a cloak that I wore, masked in sarcasm, and then was able to remove for only a little while at a time.

If you have never actually experienced depression for yourself, it can be really challenging to explain or grasp. Some people think it's a simple sadness that someone can or should "just get over" but it's truly much more than that. Depression is a constant, overwhelming, suffocating feeling that you're always trying to escape from. Recently, I saw some different depictions of those who had suffered its effects. There was an artist, a writer, and a theater producer who all seemed to have a slightly unique way of showing what one encounters with this disease.

Depression is a serious mental illness and if you know someone who is struggling with it or if you yourself are going through this, don't wait to seek out professional help. It can be hard to do this because there is a social stigma on getting help. However, this may be one of the best decisions you can make for yourself, your family, and your future. Don't give in to the lie that your family and friends will think you are crazy or that there's something wrong with you. At times, we all struggle with our mental health. You are not alone. You are not a burden. You are not a mistake. Good preventative maintenance and counseling can go such a long way toward getting stronger and recovering. Additionally, if you're the trusted friend or adult trying to help someone and worry about how they'll react, get them help nonetheless. It is better to have them mad and upset with you, than to wonder if they would be here today.

One night during the second semester of senior year, my friend Edward called the cops on me around midnight. My family was all sound asleep and I was awake texting him, casually mentioned I had a knife, and suppose the mention came off with more emphasis than any other time I'd said that before because he immediately called my phone. I did not answer. Then he tried calling the house phone but I had already unplugged it in anticipation. He proceeded to call my sister, Josie, and left a voicemail which I promptly snuck in and erased before she even woke up to see anybody called. He had one of our other friends call her too then try me. I was blocking out all the help and lifelines being thrown at me that night, trying to assure him in texts that he was the one overreacting.

Naturally, anybody would be freaked out by these comments, so he bolted to his parents' room and woke them up looking for my mom's cell phone number, frantically trying to explain what he thought was happening. They told him that he needed to call the police and send them to my house. His mom rang mine, and his dad jumped in the car to come over and check on everything in person.

I heard my mom get up a couple minutes after phones stopped ringing and knew she would be checking on me. I sprang from my closet floor where I hid the knife and quickly crawled into bed, pretending to be fast asleep. The bedroom door opened, she softly said my name once or twice, I stirred a little bit, then the door shut and she went downstairs for a drink of water, afore warned that the police were on their way to our house.

Once I heard sirens on the street behind the house, I knew it could be a late night. I grabbed the knife from the closet then crept downstairs as quickly and silently as possible. I went over to the piano and slid the knife into the bench – just in case anyone asked to search my bedroom. As I was shutting the lid of the seat, I glanced up at the window to see four beastly policemen rushing up our front lawn with their massive baton flashlights aimed at the house as they approached. I ran back upstairs instantly, without making a sound. They knocked loudly on the front door and my mom went from the kitchen to answer it.

As soon as she opened the door, they started telling her

to keep her hands in plain view and asked for me, loudly. As they asked "Does a high school girl named 'Ellie' live here, last name 'Wolf'?" I came down the stairs and joined her at the door to "innocently see who was showing up at our house so late" and was promptly pulled out onto the porch for questioning by everybody present.

Now, writing this for you four years later, I do not remember all of their questions. They were following up on everything Ed previously, frantically spewed to the dispatcher over the phone. I do distinctly remember two things: lying, and trembling while trying my best not to. When they questioned me about having a knife "in my bedroom or on my person" I could confidently and honestly respond "No, I do not" as it was now just on the other side of the front door in the piano bench. Right as the questioning finished, Ed's dad pulled up, sprinted to our porch, and gave me the biggest hug I've ever gotten from him, or possibly any person, to this day.

For a long time, I was incredibly upset with Ed for calling on me that night. After all of these intimidating strangers and his dad left our house and my mom went back to bed, I sent him the following message on Myspace saying

Ed,

Your dad came over in the middle of the night, practically crying, and gave me a hug that said "oh my gosh ellie-we-were-all-SO-unbelievaly-scared-for-you-because-ed-was-racing-around-the-house like a mad-man". PLEASE don't worry about me- like that anyways. or freak out like that. my heart is just slowing down from the cops racing up to my house with their huge flash lights and my mom opening the door and them yelling to put our hands up. my mom will prolly be tossing and turning in bed for the next three hours. but i hope your parents won't be, but your dad looked like he might and it sounded like you and your mom were in suspense over there…

i'm really really sorry about today, last week, last month, and the two years before that.

if it means anything, I love you friend…

-ellie

I don't think we talked until the next school day. The way our school was set up, students gathered only twice each week then did the work assigned for home on the other three days. Whenever the next school day was, our conversation started with the biggest hug he had ever given me and he would not let go till the second bell rang. I think it was nearly a seven-minute hug. I asked if he read the message and he said he did but wanted to respond in person. The short of it was that he cared about me so much he was not afraid to risk our friendship, knowing that my life was more valuable.

As time went on, and we moved on from that frightful night, I found a lot of solace and comfort in music. It was a means of creativity from other artists who could relate to how I felt night after night. Music can be such a powerful tool. Even now, there are songs and melodies that quickly take me back to that very dark time, when I sat on my bed drawing blood from my wrist, one line behind the next, then later tell anyone who asked about it that I was playing with my cat. These emotional triggers seem to get better and less intense over time, but I'm still amazed at the ability of the senses to overwhelm you. Much like the flowers at the funeral, the music can also be tied to bitter memories.

One day, in an attempt to express myself, I wrote the following simple lyrics and messaged them to Ed, who was a member of at least one band at any given time. He told me that he saw me in the lyrics and seemed to understand what I was trying to convey.

I Try

I try
To look him in the eye
And convince him I'm alright

He asks if I'm ok
I just fake a smile so he'll go away (for a while)
but through it he can still see me (wanting to really smile)

Chorus:
But then I start to cry
or then I start to laugh
and all I can say is, "I'll try"

I try
to show in my face
that I'm trying to get myself to a better place

He doesn't know what to think
He doesn't know what to say
other than, "Don't you dare go away"

He also wrote a song about my depression. At the time, he was in a semi-serious scream-o band and his lyrics ended up being put to music and actually recorded onto their EP. Today, I bet I am the only person who has the recording on an iPod, and he said I could share the words with you, here.

Her Secret

The knife at her throat
irritates her skin
(One slide of hand
and it's the end)
A deep breath
A second thought
(She can't do it
not tonight)

Why do we think that
we can let her do this?
Why does it take so
long to get her through this
She takes so long to
realize she can't do this
Why can't she see that
we'll all help her through this
(Sure she's got problems
but don't we all?)

She's got no reason
to take the fall
Sure she's got problems
But don't we all?
(She's got no reason
to take the fall)
The scars on her arms
reveal her secret
(they look fresh

open and bleeding)
A turned face
with blushing cheeks
(She knows we saw
her secret)

At the end of the school year, our high school sent the students from each grade on a short volunteer field trip. All year long, the students worked tirelessly to fundraise for their trip. The first trip after school was finished, was for the freshmen that would spend the week listening to sermons in the mountains and preparing the retreat center for summer campers. Then the sophomores went to one of the many orphanages just outside of Juárez, Mexico for a week to tend to maintenance jobs and play VBS games with the kids at the orphanage they visit. The juniors attended a two-week seminar near Colorado Springs on the topic of Christian worldview. Seniors had the option to go spend a week in Washington, D.C.

Since Ed was one of the only ones who knew about my depression and death fantasies, he urged me to hang tight for different upcoming events. For instance, our class trip to Mexico. He would remind me of all the fun we would have there and that it would be a great adventure. He was always looking for something to make me look forward to, hoping it would be enough to pacify my inward and downward spirally illness. By the time we were seniors, our class dwindled down to just six students. Someone jokingly suggested Hawaii as a replacement for our D.C. trip, since it was optional either way. In the end, Hawaii won! Once this trip was set in stone, Ed didn't have to persuade me to "hold on" very often, aside from the one police visit, that is.

Two days before most of our class was set to take off for the week in Hawaii, one of my friends from a different school died by suicide. His name was Peter. We knew each other through a teen group Bible study hosted at one of our friend's houses. Nobody saw his suicide coming. Neither his family nor closest friends at school even knew what he had been thinking throughout that spring of 2008. Because I was in a similar place to him mentally, I could see in his eyes—the extreme sadness, even during the few relatively short conversations we shared. He would zone out sometimes, like I would, and was always pretty quiet. I believed that he was "just shy" and I regret never talking to him about it. Even though we were not very close, I wish there was more I could have done to make a positive impact somehow, even though I wasn't in the right state of mind myself and thought I didn't have a right to pry. Hurt people cannot much help other hurt people; they often just sit there together, hurt.

All the way through my years of depression in high school, I leaned on Ed daily, which wasn't fair to him. Even if it meant calling me at one in the morning, he would, just to make sure we had checked in for the night. It was for the sake of accountability, to make sure I kept breathing, but it wasn't right for him to have picked up this responsibility as a high school student. He would tell me all the time, "Ellie, just wait until school is out for Christmas break … for summer … for the trip to Hawaii where you'll turn eighteen … for graduation … for the day you can move out of the house!" He always found something for me to hold onto, something to look forward to when I saw nothing past my wrist. Seeing firsthand the impact in my own life of both depression and losing Peter, one experience within the other, my senses sobered up rather quickly.

I missed Peter's memorial service because it happened the following week while we were on the class trip. At the service, everyone received a guitar pick, the brand he used to play with, that came with a small image of an eagle on the front, with his initials written on the back and a small card with Galatians 2:20 written on it. I was given the set later after the trip and still sport the pick often, on the chain with an angel pendant I was given the year my dad died and the little ring that says "hope." I pray for Peter's family as often as I think to, as well as all those who are battling depression alone and dealing with effects of youth suicide.

Despite what this friend did and that I wanted to do similarly to myself, I never questioned God's existence. I knew He was up in heaven, watching me slice my flesh into pieces and consume harmful substances that were never intended to be swallowed. He was up there, maybe calling out my name loudly while the angels cried, maybe crying just as much as me.

Two factors caused my depression to fester. First, I began to wonder, *what if I was in the car with my dad for the accident?* The idea was alluring. The second source was academic pressures. In school, Laine consistently scored high and teachers who had her as a student expected me to do the same, as did my parents. Complicating matters further, I grew up with an acute case of Dyslexia, which my grandma, a school psychologist, first recognized. My mom tried not to let it become a crutch for my education, but kept in mind that I would probably need extra time or help for assignments. Even so, this discouraged me from doing more reading than required for both school and entertainment.

For my case of depression, I have since admitted that it would have been much wiser to have been admitted to a hospital on suicide watch and gotten professional help. Had I not lied my way through those years and lived in my own world of denial, shame, and façades, everything could have changed earlier than it did. I could have gotten better a lot sooner. I had become so emotionless, that one night I sat on my bed with a small piece of a razor blade, etching a heart into my hip. Next to it I carved a cross, praying to God, *where is Your love?* He felt so far away, and I felt utterly alone. Another time, I spent a good hour seeing how deep I could work a clipped portion of thin, sharp metal into my skin on my left shoulder, searching for the left subclavian artery, also known as the axillary artery, to bleed it out. This is the only scar from cutting that I still have to date; Jesus has miraculously healed the rest.

I do not remember the last time I cut or inflicted self-harm, aside from the year (2009). A lot of people note the date so they can commemorate each anniversary, which is especially exciting as the years build and often from there you can love yourself better through recovery. I love reading posts online and hearing friends say, "I'm X number of years sober from self-harm today!" My heart is warmed each time someone declares victory over death.

Recovery is not a quick process, and that is ok. It can be messy, and that is ok. The goal is to believe that tomorrow may be better than today was. I recorded a few thoughts that I posted on Instagram for two years on National Suicide Prevention Day, September 10:

Being on the other side of depression for a few years, I can testify that I understand what it is like. More than severe sadness, it is a new battle every time you open your eyes. A search for hope that every tomorrow MIGHT end up better than each yesterday. You need to know that you ARE valuable & loved! Truly loved, the kind of love that is selfless—people ARE worried for you. They can tell when you lie "I'm fine" with that fake smile and it hurts them when you refuse to let them in. Scars & all, you matter. You CAN press through! (2014)

I am so glad you're reading this, know why? Because it means you're still BREATHING. Do you know what that means? That you are VALUABLE. You're valuable because you have a mind, will, & emotions, which allow you to make decisions and ENJOY life. So today— because you are breathing—decide to enjoy each breath. Then do it again tomorrow because you are precious, important, & so worth loving. (2015)

No matter how many times I tried to end my life over those three years, God continued to protect me from myself. He clearly had better plans that I wasn't yet aware of. I recently heard Bob Hazlett speak at a conference. The thing he said that stuck with me the most: "The Psalms talk about how God has always thought of you. It is true! So, when He created light on the first day of creation, in addition to Him with Jesus and Holy Spirit, you were on His mind! When He made land and separated the waters, you were on His mind!"

Chapter 4

ELLIE GOES WEST

I t was fall of 2009 and I was working as a barista and volunteer assistant director, living paycheck to paycheck in a two-room apartment with Laurene, my childhood friend. One year out of high school, we were ready for some extra freedom. Expenses were tight and I was tired of making do with little to none left over after paying rent, utilities, furniture, car insurance, gasoline, and my half of the food for each month. Moving out is more expensive than I had thought. I was getting a good taste of the real world.

One evening, I was on my way home from one of my two jobs trying to think of how I would pay all of my bills. I considered then concluded that dancing in clubs for some extra cash was my best option. I was looking for a quick way to stay afloat and independent, after recently being embarrassingly short on funds at the grocery store. When I got back home, I got out my laptop and was about to search for clubs to apply to. Instead, I first brought up my email, out of habit. There, waiting for me, was an email from my uncle in a small, California mountain town. He was asking if I'd decided to start school or was content to stay a barista through the following spring. If the plan was coffee, he suggested I consider leaving and move out to California to spend the winter working at any one of many local ski resorts near his family and North Lake Tahoe. I had roughly three weeks to think about it before our lease was up. I considered it, made pro/con lists, asked God about it, and talked it over with friends. It was clear to me that this was the best time to have a little adventure. I doubted that I would get an opportunity like this again, so a few weeks later I finished out my lease, quit the barista gig, packed my bags, and headed west.

During this transition, a week before leaving Colorado, I wrote a short note to my friends on Facebook that explained why I thought it was best for me to leave for a bit. I told them I needed a challenge, a fresh start—that my heart yearned for adventure, and perhaps make a few mistakes and learn from them. I wasn't mad at anyone; I just needed a change and a chance to expand my horizons.

After arriving in California, I crashed at my grandmother's house a couple hours' drive away. During those first few weeks I really hit the ground running and attended three different job fairs, each at a different resort. The first was pretty organized, the second was too crazy and packed to even get an interview, and the third ran so behind schedule that by the time I was up for an interview most of the staff were too exhausted to interview anyone else. Luckily, the first resort offered me a position as "lead coffee cart barista" working through the food and beverage department in the main lodge. I moved into staff housing the week of Thanksgiving and started before the season began.

A handful of us jumped in early to help with cleaning off summer dust and prepping the kitchen. After living on the summit for a couple of weeks, the housing units were full of a couple hundred employees, a mix of locals and foreigners. My reputation of "the innocent, Christian girl from Colorado" quickly spread and I didn't mind. I enjoyed being gawked at because I was different in good ways and tried my best to be a representation of the deep-seated convictions I was raised with. I took pride in my identity as the innocent, Christian girl.

I was once told by one of the mountain guys, "Everyone else who lives here gets down. Everyone else smokes weed. Everyone else drinks. How and why are you living here?" He was genuinely hoping for an answer. At the time, evangelism was not my strong suit. I told him I would write down his question and take it to heart so I could form a complete and honest response and get back to him. I did it this way so I would not leave anything out.

Here's what I came up with to share the following day:

I am living here to set an example, to be a living example of Christ, to be a light. I'm also here because I want to grow, to learn and to experience new things. Taking the weekends to get drunk and high isn't something that I have any interest in, because I don't think it's good for me or for my body. I moved out here to grow up and stop living in the past and to witness through my lifestyle and have my life wrecked, in a good way, all with God.

I am not here to belong or fit in, for most that's what high school was for. I have to be okay with being slightly uncomfortable where I am, while being comfortable in my skin. I am not here to force my relationship with God on anybody. I am here to meet new people and leave a good impression. Mostly, I am here because I believe it's where God wants me to be.

Try as I might to put God first, I soon realized it's true that "bad company corrupts good character" (1 Corinthians 15:33). Instead of spending more of my quiet mornings and evenings in the Word, my focus shifted entirely into making friends above any other goals. Looking back, it sometimes feels like wasted opportunities that I could have spent with the Lord, learning and growing and sharing from a place of intentionally cultivated intimacy with Him. There is purpose in being social, but I allowed it to dictate all my free time. I just pray that any of the people who are still in contact will see how He has transformed me. When they knew me, I had caved in on most of my morals. We dressed scantily, went to huge parties with lots of booze, and did things we shouldn't have. And what pains me is that it was *my* choice.

If you watch snow fall, sometimes you see snowflakes on their way to the ground and think you can predict precisely where each will land. But then a cross breeze sweeps in and adds a few extra loops into the equation and totally changes the course. This is the visual in my life then. The cross breeze represents influential friends, the extra loops represents activities that take one off course, and the snowflake represents me while living in this place. I allowed my spiritual life to become so mundane while trying to appease my housemates because I wanted to earn the "right" to influence them. I was attempting to walk in the lifestyle of partiers to grow friendships or relationships with the goal of introducing them to Christ, but I was not representing Him the correct way to anybody. There were times I could not joyfully serve customers on an exceedingly rough day because I hadn't prioritized connecting with Jesus and receiving His life. My spirit cried out for the Lord, to be with Him again, but I silenced this cry with busyness.

Culture will win you over if you are not consistently grounded in Christ. When you think you are solid enough to try to "win souls for the Kingdom" on your own, you still need more of Him. If you think you're full of the Holy Spirit, double check your heart from time to time for wrong judgments toward your housemates, neighbors, and coworkers. Stay plugged in with the Lord, regardless of how tired you become. Rest in Him. Looking on it now, this would have saved me so much grief and hardship later on.

Our department managers sometimes hung out with us after work. We would go see movies, have game nights, or head to parties. We all got pretty good at dancing in tightly packed rooms and playing common team games such as "beer pong" and "flip cup." Once, I walked into work and, realizing I was still drunk from the previous night of shenanigans, told my boss before he figured it out.

"Ellie, I'm so proud of you!" he said, high-fiving me. "Be sure you don't burn yourself on the coffee machine."

Underage drinking was the "biggest" civil law I broke while living in California, next to obtaining one speeding ticket. It was clear from my early teenage years, and talks with my mom, that I wouldn't have sexual relations prematurely. When I was thirteen, my mom sat me down for a heart-to-heart about abstinence, which I was thankful for. I was strongly in agreement with the decision to "save myself for marriage." Attending the *Pure by Choice* rally twice in the following few years was somewhat helpful, but at the same time fed my naivety. I understood that I shouldn't have sex outside of marriage, but no one explicitly taught me what sex was, what abstinence looked like, or *why* it mattered so much. The little I remembered from fifth grade sexual education was the 101 on periods and the stages of growth of a baby in the womb.

A parent's job is to "raise their children in the way they should go" (Proverbs 22:6). I believe this means they should make things black and white, wrong and right. As awkward as conversations may become, I strongly advise *to leave no gray area.* Talk thoroughly about the negative, addictive, mental, and physical effects of excessive masturbation and any consumption of pornography. Talk about how tightly intertwined the pornography/sex industry is tied to human sex trafficking (resources for this information can be found at the end of this book). Talk with your kids about the things you wish you knew and should have known at their age and allow room in the conversation for them to ask questions at any time. Remind them there is always freedom to say "no" and if anyone disrespects the lack of consent, even for a hug, then that person is in the wrong. Teach them how to respond to violation. Let them know your regrets and mistakes, at age-appropriate levels. Things may get squeamish, but this is vital as they head into "the real world" and leave the protective love bubble you raised them in. Don't let these questions be answered by friends at school, or even youth group. The chances are good that their friends from school will offer distorted and incomplete views, especially if their parents are not having conversations with them on these matters, either. Youth groups tend to presume that you have taught them more than you have, and do not cover enough. So, speak up. Begin these conversations about honoring others and oneself well while they are young and have them often.

Entering my teenage years with overwhelmingly low self-esteem largely fed by verbal abuse proved to be a perfect storm. Two of my guy friends continually harassed me to send dirty photos via text message. They tried to justify their requests with things like "if we are really friends, you would send me a shot," "picture for picture," or "I'll show as little or much as you show me." This lasted about a year all told and I was not the only young girl they were requesting from. When any of us spoke up and tried to get the issue addressed, most adults did not believe us because of who the boys were in the community. Anyone who did could only ask either boy if it was true, they denied it, and that was that. Then they laughed at us for trying to find help. Up until I moved to California, this was the greatest challenge I faced when it came to the promise

I made to God, my mom, and myself to remain "pure" for my future husband.

Once my ski-bum friends and neighbors found out I was nineteen and had not really been in a relationship their jaws dropped—especially the guys. It first came out at a Thanksgiving dinner that was being hosted at a nearby house. It was convenient for those of us who were new to the area, or those whose families lived far enough away that they didn't have time to go visit them and be back at work the next day. A handful of us walked over together, introductions were made, and we were given a brief tour of the deck, complete with a special notation of the keg in the corner. I ended up chatting with three guys, two of which knew each other well from previous seasons working at this same ski resort. Since there was a large keg in the corner, the guys kept going back to it with their red solo cups to get refills. They offered to fill a cup for me, and I responded, "No thanks; I'm only nineteen." They laughed, obviously baffled by my ignorance because no one cares if you're of age; after all, it's a summit party!

Through the night, the conversation shifted and they learned that I had moved from Colorado. One of them asked if I had a boyfriend waiting for me back there. I told them I didn't, which prompted them to ask further questions.

"But, you have been kissed … right?"

I told them the truth. "Um, not on the lips."

All three stood there in silence for a minute and stared at me with puzzled looks. Eventually, one pieced it together and exclaimed, "WAIT, so … that means you've never had sex, either?!"

I just laughed and shook my head.

Still puzzled, he continued, "How could anyone make it this long and still abstain?"

I told them I'm a Christian and believe that sex was designed for a man and woman who are married to each other.

They accepted that and said, "Wow, well, you're really strong then!"

The ski season ran from the end of November of 2009 to the end of April the following year. As I left work on the evening of April 7, 2010, my manager told me if I would like to get more hours I could come in at 7:00 am the next morning, an hour and a half before I was scheduled.

"Thanks, see you tomorrow!" I replied as I headed back to staff housing. Since it was late in the season, both of my roommates had left. Those of us who were still there were celebrating a friend's birthday that evening, so I changed out of my work clothes and headed to the party. When I arrived, I found cans of cheap beer and some sort of whiskey for all to share. I only had one can and two shots over the course of several hours—you know, because I was trying to be responsible since I had an opening shift the next morning. It wasn't unlike most parties I had been to up until this point, but things quickly began to move in a different direction. Someone was openly dealing out hard party drugs. He had quite a stash, it seemed. I had never seen this take place before; I had only heard about it. Two friends of mine were taking hit after hit after hit. It was some form of ecstasy, and the dealer was offering it to everyone. I was quick to turn it down, using the "early morning shift" excuse to mask my disinterest. I wasn't about to throw out the few remaining rules I had for myself with just under a month remaining in this job, but nobody there was mad or cared that I passed the offer.

It was kind of fascinating for me to be in the room to observe everyone. There is something alluring about drugs because of their powerful effect. Since I didn't know much about ecstasy, I thought the side effects would be similar to marijuana—they would quickly pass out and we would all see each other at work the next day, like the rest of the season. Apparently, that is not how the drug works. Instead, two of its main side effects are a sharper awareness of senses and a heightened sexual drive.

Shortly after midnight, things began to quiet down as people dispersed one by one. Between wishing a final "happy birthday" to the honoree and excusing myself for the night, I asked around if anyone else had to head to work early the next morning, trying to find a fallback in case I slept through my alarm. One of the heavily drugged guys said he had to be up early. I thought that was a little odd, since he did a great number of lines that night. As he was the only one who offered, I asked if he would knock on my door when he woke up around 5:30 or 6:00 to ensure I did not oversleep. In return, I offered him a ride into work so he wouldn't have to walk the three miles before the sun was up. He quickly agreed and I went back to my room.

Around 4:15, he knocked on my door. I checked the time on my phone, confused as to why he was over an hour early. I opened the door to find him utterly delirious.

"Hey, why are you here so early?" I asked, trying to not be blinded by the hallway light.

"Three other people are passed out on my bed. Do you have space in here?"

I gestured to one of the two empty beds and said he could use that for the rest of the night as long as we still woke up for work on time. I went to grab some blankets for him off my bed, still half asleep. I'm not sure if he heard me on the spare bed thing or if he simply chose not to hear me but, like a lost puppy, he followed me into my bed.

"No, there's a spare bed over there. You're not sleeping with me," I replied, pointing again to the spare beds. It was no use. He was drugged, and we were exhausted. I wasn't comfortable with him in my bed, but I began to fall back asleep within a few moments so I wasn't too concerned as long as he did the same. Logic told me that nothing bad would happen if we were both sleeping and, at that point while consistently working over-time, sleep was sleep.

My voice still quivers at times when I talk about what happened next.

Drifting in and out of sleep, I began to wake again when I realized he was being super chatty. I had no idea what he was saying; I just wanted him to stop talking so I could go to sleep. Moments later, he began to touch me lightly. At that point, I knew sleep was no longer an option so I began to engage him in conversation—trying to distract him. Chatting led to him touching me more vigorously, which led to him kissing me, which led to a slight of his hands. Since my morals had slid with others before this point I was not too worried about making this guy stop when I was uncomfortable. A big tendency I saw there was that people would rather not care about rules and morals when it comes to emotion, people want to fit in and to feel accepted. My remaining rules were simple, no drugs aside from alcohol and my pants *will* always stay on. I am proud to report that I still have never tried drugs. However, "pants" was sometimes interchanged to "underwear" and "stay on" in this case was twisted as I was forcibly told, "It is still *on* ... just lower ... near your knees." Less than amused, I did my best to stay as clothed as possible. I struggled for over an hour, to no avail, with verbal protest and repeated attempts to re-dress myself, but he had his way with me. He was a strong guy. I should have kicked him or screamed, but remember being too afraid of not being heard and not knowing what he would do if I called for help. I didn't want to make things worse, so I kept quiet aside from petition while he did what he wanted. He repeatedly responded to my "No, stop!" with "But doesn't this feel so good?"

Finally, I told him for the second or third time that I was late for work and reminded him that was the only reason he was there in the first place. This seemed to be the first thing he actually "heard," as he finally let up and got off of me. As quickly as possible, I rolled off my bed and got ready for work. What I wanted most was to shower, but since I was already late I quickly dressed, brushed my teeth, pulled my hair back, and ran. He silently sat at the foot of my bed, puzzled and dazed, while I rushed about getting ready. I told him to leave, twice; but he just asked if we could talk.

At a loss for words I stammered, "You want to *talk*?

Seriously?! Argh, fine, but not right now. You know I'm already an hour late! Don't you have to go in, too?!"

He shot me a quick, smug smile.

I was beyond disgusted.

He was supposed to knock on my door, make sure I was up, then leave till we rode into work. Instead, he came in, laid down next to me, and began talking so I couldn't fall back asleep.

He was *only* supposed to be sure I was awake for work, but instead, he kissed me.

He was supposed to make sure I was dressed for work, but instead, he ripped my clothes off of me.

He was supposed to make sure I was up for work, but instead, he raped me.

After I left for work, this guy disappeared for four days coming down from his high and then we tried talking but nothing productive came from the conversation. Not even an apology.

By the time I finally made it in to work that morning, the manager had nearly completed all of the opening tasks. I wasn't late for my original shift, but had showed up between my original starting time and the time I had agreed to come in early.

"Do you need the tills over there?" he asked, noticing I was trying to figure out what remained to be done.

I hurriedly said, "Yes, that'd be great!" and went with him to retrieve them from the office.

"Sorry I was late," I began, pausing to see how he would respond.

He checked his watch and replied, "Oh, I hadn't even

noticed. Thanks for still coming in a little early!" He didn't ask if I overslept my alarm. He did not ask anything! Why would he? Part of me was relieved.

What I said before about having a reputation on a small summit like this one is that even the managers talk. If he knew what had happened just before, there could be no end of comments related to my faith, my overall behavior, and a questioning of the goodness of God. On the other hand, now I see that him asking should have been welcomed on my end. Identifying and processing the situation would have resolved it quicker and better than it ever was. I imagine that, as both a decent guy and a manager, he would have offered to or been required report the incident, whereas I was too traumatized to even consider it.

No further discussion was had about what may or may not have happened the night before, and I hid in my coffee corner making drinks the rest of the day. I felt ashamed, sick, and absolutely horrible for the entire nine-hour workday, my hands trembling with every cup of coffee I prepared. Terrified my abuser would come into the lodge for whatever reason.

When I was finally able to meet with two other friends that evening who were not at the party the night before, I told them what happened. Their feedback was, "Oh great! Now you know what sex is like and won't be wondering anymore …" and, "It was awful, wasn't it? Nothing too special." and even, "See, what did I tell you? Totally not something to look forward to on the honeymoon once you get married, right?"

In retrospect, my friends' advice was horrible. They listened, sort of, but turned around and belittled the weight of the situation. Someone should have known or told me that you are supposed to go to the cops as soon as possible and file a police report within 24 hours. You should not shower, or clean any of your sheets or clothing. You need to turn in everything for evidence along with a report of the event. This may have been touched on for half a second in middle or high school, but since it is such an uncomfortable subject, most teachers, youth group leaders, and parents try to avoid it altogether, doubting anything bad will ever happen to their children. Perhaps my friends did not know these things, either.

On that April day, I had absolutely no idea what to do. I felt gross, nasty, unworthy of anything good, uncomfortable, disgusting, and personally disgusted—even after I finally had the chance to take a hot shower after work that evening. I was late for my opening shift, which ultimately was how I got out of the situation, together with a hundred "no's" and "please stops." My body mostly shut down part way through, once the brain realized there was not relief on the way. This guy I barely knew was sexually abusing me and I was pretty sure that had never happened to me before; I did not know what to do. I heard somewhere that "my body is my body" and "no means no," but he was not hearing it then.

I was talking about all of this with a friend a few weeks later with the theory in mind that I was raped because I had drifted from the strong relationship I had with God, that it was somehow *my* fault. I reasoned that God did not stop my rapist, but was watching and probably upset with both the guy and myself, but then He quickly used the situation for my good to draw me back to Him. To put it simply, I felt like being raped was a punishment from God for my own wandering and poor choices.

I now understand this is *not* what happened, and it is not the heart of God! It was my neighbor's choice to use drugs and then to act on the side effects. I was simply in the wrong place at the wrong time. I was so upset with the situation and myself. For so long, I felt a deep sense of shame, as if it were entirely my fault that it happened. This was something to be processed externally just as much as internally. Your mind plays tricks on you and says "what if?" but the truth always comes out. This is not something to keep a secret. Speak truth until someone listens, believes you, and can help you get professional help, which leads to healing.

I forgave my friends for not telling me what I *should* have done, and hope that if this ever happens to someone I know and they come to me, I'll be able to get them to the police station or a hospital to take the appropriate steps right away, if they can report. There are a lot of variables on this—mostly emotional and mental—but, ultimately, I advise it to be the best option, as it could stop the abuser from continuing to abuse others.

From my experience, once one has come to terms with the fact that they have been raped, it is really hard *not* to tell everyone they know. This isn't so much because they are searching for pity from others. It's not that they're trying to forever be the victim and garner sympathy. They need to find someone—anyone—who can relate to the situation and obscure emotions that go with it, someone who can usher in healing.

Along the way, I have learned there are many people who do not need to know this about me. Now, in sharing so openly here, the entire world could know in a matter of seconds. Because of the call for transparency on my life, I have shared my full story with both male and female friends when we swap life stories as well as in seminar settings as anecdotes while teaching. As a caveat, I would advise not to share these kinds of deep, personal events unless you fully trust the person with whom you're conversing. This sentence gave me such a freedom when a therapist validated this: you do not need to disclose everything about your past before you start dating somebody. There is freedom for healthy boundaries and a need-to-know basis as relationships progress. The more you are able to healthily talk about it with trusted friends or a good counselor, the more you can potentially remember and be able to process healthily over time.

Some of my friends, who did not initially understand this, asked me, "Wait, but you said this other thing last time we talked about it!" and "Why are you changing your story, again?!" I tried to explain that, as time passed and I further processed what had taken place, I was able to remember more details of the horrid event that were initially lodged who-knows-where in my brain. Not getting help or appropriate closure after being raped, the entire three-hour event went into my repressed memory by the time I moved back to Colorado a month later. There it resided, unlabeled and untouched, for seven months before it was somehow brought to the forefront of my mind. It truly was a nightmare, that came in pieces over a couple months of conversations and many, many cups of tea. Someone in this position needs a friend who will listen as words slowly come and who will simply hold them, expecting nothing in return.

As if these California months weren't eventful enough, I

was talking on the phone with one of my siblings, Ken, who told me that our stepdad had moved to a different state over the winter for a job. Apparently, he had begun dating another woman and had filed for divorce from our mom.

After I hung up the phone, I went out onto the balcony with my friends, who sat bundled up in the cold, smoking cigarettes. I reiterated the news that my brother had just told me, mostly in shock that it was finally happening—after I begged her to file so many times during high school, because of the way he treated us for so long.

A few of them said, "Wow, I'm so sorry, Ellie." Others simply said, "Welcome to the club" and offered me drags to help calm my nerves as I processed the news. I declined, but if there had ever been a moment for me to try cigarettes for myself, it would have been then.

At season's end, a friend from Denver flew out to help me move home. We took the long way through Oregon, over to Montana, and down I-25 through Wyoming, staying with friends and family the whole way.

A week and a half after moving back home, I wrote this piece as I began to settle back into life in Denver.

"Home is the place you grow up wanting to leave, and grow old trying to get back to." ~ John Ed Pearce

Home is the place that bores you the most.
Home is where you had your first pet.
Home can be any house where you feel comfortable enough to open the fridge without being invited to do so.
Home is where you chill & relax.

Home is where you go when you are finished running around town.

Home is the most familiar or comforting scent in your life.

Home is the one pile of sticks, bricks, or plywood you will never forget your way to.

Home once was your sanctuary; the walls knew all of your secrets & talents.

Home is where you and your best friends have memories in every corner of every room on every floor, and the stairs.

Home is where you hide in your closet listening to your iPod as loud as you can while your parents are "discussing loudly" down the hallway.

Home might be the last place you would like to be right now.

Home is where you know everybody and everybody knows you, probably more than you would all care to.

Home is where you tried to ride a bike for the first time with your dad.

Home is where you "helped out" your mom in the kitchen by burning the toast, but she smiled, scraped it, and then ate it anyways.

Home is where you held your new baby brother or sister every day while mom made lunch for you.

Home is where you run to when you need to get away, for free.

Home is where you made forts.

Home is where you decorated the entire front porch,

driveway, and sidewalk with chalk... then brushed your hands off on the lawn before being allowed back inside again.

No matter where you are in life...

No matter what you have or have not done with your life...

No matter how far away you are...

...your home will always be there.

...your family will always support and accept you.

...Once you get within thirty miles, home will never be hard to find.

Being home has a way of reconnecting you with your true self. In those still moments at home, I realized I had crossed some boundaries—not only with alcohol, but with boys. On top of that, I couldn't remember the last time I'd opened the Bible I used to read every day. It was like a dusty piano, sitting dormant and untuned in the corner of a room. In the past, almost every list I made would begin with a bullet point about my Savior or a Scripture, but lately that bullet didn't even make the list. I was struggling with the regret and consequences of poor choices (mine and others').

Chapter 5

MISSIONS

When I returned home to Colorado, I began rekindling old friendships, as well as my relationship with the Lord. Having been out of state for only seven months, most friendships picked up where we left off. I was working as a coordinator at a summer camp with one of the theater companies I had worked with before, and started attending church again regularly. Within a few Sundays of being back, there was an announcement about a short-term mission trip to South Africa. It sounded amazing! It was arranged for these two weeks of work to be covered for me to go with the blessing and encouragement of my boss, and I did.

This was my first time flying trans-Atlantic. Our team flew from Denver. to Washington, D.C., to Senegal, and on to Johannesburg, South Africa. From there, we drove for an hour and a half before arriving at a property that consisted of a house, two guest houses, a large yard, and a children's shelter where our church's resident missionary family lived and worked. There was an eight-hour time difference between Colorado to South Africa. After all of that travel, I showered, crashed in my bed, and was up by 8:00 the next morning. This was my first time experiencing substantial jetlag. The first half of that week was a blur, full of slurred and sleep deprived words, and, obviously, lots of coffee.

While traveling abroad, I learned more about other cultures. For instance, in South Africa when you meet someone you show thumbs up, pound it, then press and twist your thumb off of theirs and say "sharp, sharp." With their accents, this sounds like "shop, shop." The English "thank you" there is "danky" or "donky." In both, and various other phrases, the vowel sound is a mix between the "a" and the "o."

Rustenburg was only my "home" for two weeks in 2010. I hadn't even been back in the States for three full weeks when I began to feel very homesick, which I didn't think was possible since I had been overseas for such a short time. The bruises on my shins from playing with the children may have faded, but I still had some kind of stomach bug and a relatively minor case of ringworm on my right arm. To most people, this would seem like such an inconvenience, but it awakened me to how fortunate and blessed we are in the States to have such easy access to healthcare (at the time I wrote this, I was young enough to be covered by my mother's healthcare plan).

I learned that the kids of the villages are so wanting of attention and love. They will rush out of school from the vans and see you sitting down and start jumping on you and toppling over them, trying to play. The children will climb over you, without hesitation, and sometimes bury you alive, so you have to be careful when you play with them. But they have so much love in their hearts; their smiles and laughter were such a healing balm to my heart. Without knowing it, the children were able to connect with me because we all experienced less than ideal childhoods. Also, Jesus. I started to find myself getting "me" and the past winter in California off my mind, paying more attention to them and their world.

We mostly volunteered in an area that is a well-known AIDS affected squatter camp, which means the community is not recognized by the government as a colony, meaning there is not enough aid to treat everybody with the disease. One day, we did a photo shoot for the community. With donated "point and shoot" cameras, two of us gave photography lessons to a handful of the teenagers who helped us with the photo project. They had a blast! For many in the community, this was the only photo they ever had of themselves or their families. Some had never used a mirror either, so it was so fun to see their reactions upon receiving the prints.

Some of the teammates built three metal shacks for pre-selected people of the community. The first shack our team built was for a man, his wife, their two daughters, and their little boy. I believe the caretakers told us that the whole family was HIV-positive. The second shack was for a girl who was my age and only had her little sister and brother who she took care of. Their mother had recently died, leaving them with nothing more than each other. The rest of our team members had a chance to help build the third shack because it was in the fenced-in area next to the garden that our "garden team" dug up for the community to develop. This one was for a single man who stepped up as a volunteer to watch over the garden as it flourishes, to ensure that nobody breaks in and steals everything at night. We left a bag of food and a jug of cleaner tap water at each shack when we handed over the keys and prayed over the recipients as a full team with neighbors. Every time I think about that day in the middle of the second week of our trip, I am amazed with how people make so much of so little. I wish it were "easier" to live like that here in the States and stand out in our communities in that way. We all have enough energy, time, and food in our kitchens to stay home from school or work for more than a full day and not worry. The children I met on this trip are fed typically once a day and given candy by visiting "acuñas," which is what they call white people because it means "pineapple." Children who do not know what a television is, can draw, color, play, dance, or find other ways to self-entertain better than most modern five-year-olds in America who I know.

The caretakers in the village are a handful of Catholic Sisters who volunteer with the community. They toured us around "the park," as it is referred to, and pointed out homes where they were aware of all sorts of situations. One such account was there are many grandmothers who are their grandchildren's guardians because the middle generation has died, most commonly from HIV and AIDS. We were told that people in these situations have no income because there is an influx of immigrants to this northern territory of the country who are all looking for work in the mining caves. Between losing your children and being put in charge of the grandkids who are too young to work to help financially, many grandparents find themselves in a tough position. As horrible as it is, these grandparents would often become very desperate, as food was scarce making ends meet was all one could do week after week. Many times, they'd sell off their grandkids or even grandbabies (as young as two or three years old) to neighbors for sex, just to try to feed each person who lived in their house one more time. As if the conditions aren't horrific enough, the local water is not clean enough to drink. Without any other options, the villagers had no other choice but to drink it and become horribly sick. As I took in my surroundings I stopped caring about the dirty air that turned a tissue black when I blew my nose.

We also met another woman at a different site who has a home over in Phokeng. This woman was such an inspiration, as she feeds around twenty children every day after they get out of school. After she feeds them, they come to hang out with each other at her home where they play soccer, Legos, and crafts. Since we left, they have also started a Bible study and lessons on good virtues.

We also spent some time loving on the babies at the shelter where we were staying with our resident missionary family from our church.

While visiting Johannesburg on a day without plans, we enjoyed eating crocodile, zebra, impala, and giraffe at a local tourist restaurant after getting to pet a giraffe and adolescent lions.

After two weeks in South Africa, I appreciated the United States all the more. At the time, I thought our "worst" parts of town are much cleaner and safer than many parts of the world, though I have since learned that this isn't always the case.

I realized on this mission trip how small I really am. While I can do *some* things to change the world, I'm just one person. In South Africa, I realized that participating in some seemingly simple and non-essential activities with some children at a remote village really does change their world—if only for a moment. Swinging a child around in a circle by their arms and seeing them smile, laugh, and scream with delight may just be one less minute they are thinking about their troubles and traumas. It's one less moment to think back on the scene of their shack being broken into, torn apart, and watching their mother, big sister, or baby brother being raped the night before. Suddenly, after spending time with them and getting a peek inside their world, I came to terms with how bad some have it and how grateful I am that I have been blessed with so much. This breaks my heart.

Two months after this trip to South Africa, I wrote down this note of gratitude:

I'm currently finding myself incredibly thankful tonight. I'm thankful ...

For soap :)

For a boss who likes my ideas, even at 11:30 p.m. on a Saturday night

For friends who request a text from me letting them know I made it home alright

For friends who will put a conversation on pause just to remind me that they love or miss me

For my best friend who will chill and just listen to me go
on and on about South Africa and how I am so excited
to go back next summer with my church—even though
he knows I hope to stay there for a lot, lot longer than I
went for this year.

For friends who love to be as impulsive as I am

For the friend who will have meltdown talks with me in a
car for an hour and a half during a busy week when we
both should be sleeping

For kids & teens who realize how much hard work really
does pay off

For music that someone else wrote that explains
EXACTLY what you're thinking but you couldn't find a
way to word

For music that you manage to put down in ink after being
in writer's block for what seems like ages

That I (kind of) know how to use my camera and play my
piano, much less even have those things

That I know what I have enough passion for the rest of my
life

That God has been helping me learn patience over the
course of about two years

That God has given me a CRAZY story (so far) that I am
getting better at sharing with people who are supposed
to hear it ...

To be able to see the BEAUTIFUL downtown lights and
stars from the mountains that always put a smile on

my face when I have to go out driving to relieve stress
For the ability to run

For dancing, driving with the window down and/or singing
in the rain and having my day made

Basically ... God is fan.freaking.tastic!

~ Ellie, 10/17/10

The following year, my stepdad's divorce from my mom was finalized. Between 2010 and 2011, my time was spent living at home (since he was gone) and continuing to work with the theater group. I was teaching the basics to kids between the ages of four and seven—dancing, singing, and acting. We had a showcase for their parents at the end of each ten-week session. The first session, I taught the kids a few numbers I choreographed from various *VeggieTales* episodes. In the winter, we did swing dancing, and in the spring we did *Stomp*-style routines that I choreographed, mainly focused on inclusivity between peers, and was so impressed by how much the kids learned and grew together. Receiving positive feedback from other students, staff, and parents was an extra perk. Kids are smart, capable, and don't need things to be super simple *all* of the time. Sometimes, all a discouraged or distracted child needs is for someone to look them in the eyes, and say, "Hey kid, you have great ideas and are talented. I promise that if we all practiced these moves a few more times together, you will get it down and it will be awesome!"

During the winter session, my memories of being raped began to resurface and I started to process it with a handful of my closest friends and co-workers. In the midst of this, I found both teaching and directing to be a beautiful distraction. Being a young director who balanced three classes and oversaw a show with a cast of approximately eighty students, sleep was a limited resource. I lost my voice for a week during rehearsals and took notes all over my hand. I had really hoped to make a difference in the lives of these children. But honestly, it was a challenge for me to be able to address each of my cast members individually to the degree I had hoped, though I did my best to make each one feel seen, affirmed, and valued.

While teaching and directing full-time the following spring (2011), I was convinced by the close friends I was confiding in that I needed to let my mom know I had been raped back in California. (The only thing more challenging for me besides going to her for that conversation is actually letting her read this book, if she is able to; there is a lot on these pages for a mother to learn all at once.) Our relationship has definitely grown stronger as of late since I'm the only one living at home these days, while writing, but back then I can't say it was that great. Even so, I remember her response to what I shared with her. She was a mix of disappointment, guardedness, and offense for my behalf, but also may have wanted to find and lock up the guy herself. She said I should go to the doctor, even though a full year had passed, as well as consider attending five counseling sessions covered by insurance through her work benefits. At first, I was strongly opposed to both suggestions, thinking my friends helped me do enough processing and that if I didn't notice any physical irregularities by then that everything was most likely fine. Within a couple weeks I conceded to both ideas, mostly to calm her nerves.

For the most part, my experience with the specific counselor I landed with left me more emotional and recklessly aggravated. She did her best in those visits. She specialized more in helping families and children, so I did not feel much progress in my healing journey after any given session.

All through this year, Laurene heard all of my stories about South Africa multiple times. It just so happened that one of her uncles is a pastor and lives in Zimbabwe with his wife and children. They had moved there thirty-five years before, shortly after they were married. Since then, they have built up a large church that hosts tons of awesome classes and functions. They also have a restaurant and school that sit on the same piece of land. Laurene proposed the idea of us going overseas for an extended visit to volunteer. We both got permission from our parents and contacted her uncle. Two days after the spring show I directed closed, my best friend, her mom, and I took off to spend an entire month in Zimbabwe!

Every day, I got to go to the school with Laurene's two youngest cousins, who were then fourteen and eighteen, and hung out with the four youngest classes as an aide for the teachers. I loved it! I was able to help the teachers do things too, like watch the kids during recess. The kids asked me to play soccer, read them stories, and swing them around by the arms at any free moment. I really liked their school because it seemed so much more structured than most I've seen here in the States. For example, when anybody walks into a classroom that is from an older grade or administration or a visitor, all the students stand up and welcome you in unison. It is interesting to note how much more respect they are seemingly brought up with compared to other kids of the same age I have spent time with in schools elsewhere.

Laurene, who was then studying pre-med, got to work in a government hospital and shadowed a brilliant doctor her family knows. This man was one inspiring, generous, and awesome man. He lived in his office at this hospital where he saw forty-five patients on his daily rounds and made approximately $300/month. He owned exactly two outfits, and you would never see him stop work for any sort of break during work hours – which he consistently extended. He has been recognized as the man who runs the world's largest psychosocial network, which is composed of roughly 15,000 young people globally who are infected or affected by HIV/AIDS. Whenever he is given a new pair of reading glasses, which he needs, he'll find someone within ten minutes who "needs them more." He has been given a house and an apartment but allows the orphans from the support group to live in them and pays out of pocket for their transportation to and from the local group meetings.

The group leaders he oversaw threw him a surprise Father's Day party one evening and invited us to attend. People were giving speeches, and it was truly one of the sweetest times we spent there. In one of his humble spiels, the doctor said, "If there was one thing I could change about myself, it is that I wish I could be less prideful."

We were amazed at how he barely received compliments, but of course God sees the heart. If you try to tell him how grateful you are for your time learning from him or how much he has impacted your life, he turns the conversation around in an instant and showers you with compliments. But he would always gently urge us to do stuff we didn't think we ever could, like pray for strangers, which forced us to learn to how trust God more. This is when my evangelical side began to take root.

I started to see many moves of God while in Africa. On our final Sunday at the church, I saw a woman next to me get slain in the Holy Spirit. I listened to God when He said, "Put your hand on her shoulder and ask Me to *give her more.*" I acted in obedience and was amazed at God's love, yet again. An hour later, I met with three pastors to learn more about praying in the Spirit, commonly known as the gift of tongues, discussed with other gifts throughout 1 Corinthians, which I found myself speaking before we left the meeting. During the month, these pastors also helped walk me through more healing pertaining to losing my dad and being raped. We met for coffee and processed through each incident. I found it to be easier than expected, as I shared these two specific stories for the first time with people I didn't know very well.

We later went to Victoria Falls for a short holiday. It was so beautiful! While visiting, I bungee jumped off the bridge in a harness tied at my waist, falling more than three hundred and sixty feet in a few seconds (which was completely terrifying but super fun!). We also went on a few safaris in the jungle and stayed in tree houses. We got to eat fun things like ostrich, crocodile, warthog, deep fried worms, kudu, ox, and impala. We then went back to Harare for a week and traveled home with long layovers to tour parts of Paris, France and London, England.

Laurene and I came home from Africa starving for more outreach opportunities and chances to touch lives. We had been giving so much spiritually in that time and were not ready to settle back into our routines of school and work. It just so happened within that week the city of Minot, North Dakota had a flood and our church was sending a small team up for the week to help gut houses with Samaritan's Purse. We both jumped at the opportunity to go. I was able to pull it off, but she unfortunately had to stay home since she was unable to get her shifts covered at work so last minute.

This was my least costly mission trip because each team member paid an eighth of the total price of transport. Everything we ate was donated to the church we were set up in and we slept on the floor or on cots so everything was simple overall. The first project my team worked on was the flooded basement of an 83-year-old woman. She had already gotten a good deal of the work done by her son and daughter-in-law, so we demolished her basement down to the concrete walls and support beams. Six hours after arriving, we were finished. Little did we know this would be our "easy" house.

Over the next two days, we worked on another house that was located in the part of town that was hit the hardest by flooding. To put it into perspective, the team before us had thirty volunteers working on it for over a day and still didn't have this house done. We all had to wear work boots, Tyvek suits, safety glasses, rubber gloves layered under work gloves, and a hard hat just to enter the house because it was full of black mold due to sewage residue and water that had been sitting in the house since the flood. The men went to work in the basement while the women and children worked on the main level, where the flood waters had almost reached the ceiling.

The lady who owned the house had been renting out rooms in the basement as a means of income. Some members of our team found pornographic material down there while tearing out drywall and sawing fridges and furniture in half in order to get them upstairs and out to the curb. We all got together and prayed for whoever owned the material, the lady whose house it was, and anyone who had seen it.

Later that day, one of the woman's grandsons came by the house with his wife to help with the cleanup efforts. He wanted to salvage as many memories as possible and get the house back to normal so it could stay in the family. They both accepted Christ by the end of the day.

The whole week after we got back to Denver, I was craving more of that house-gutting manual labor so badly, that I considered going back for a longer time to help more. I wasn't able to do so, because I was set to move a month later to Madison, Wisconsin for a six-month Discipleship Training School at the YWAM base. I was drawn to this specific non-profit mission base because it runs schools with an emphasis on outreach to women and children around the world who suffer from or are at major risk of poverty and abuse. The school started with three months of intensive training in the context of close-knit, Christian community. Our school was composed of twenty-eight girls and just five boys. There were about ten girls per room, five boys in one room, and a "no dating people in the school" policy. This prevented cliques in smaller groups of friends and kept us focused throughout our short time there. Each week we had different speakers lined up to share with us on various topics, which included: Hearing God's voice, keeping a clean conscience, learning how to intercede, the fear of the Lord, faith, relationships, the Kingdom of God, the father heart of God, roots of pride and humility, spiritual warfare, the role of the Holy Spirit, our divine destinies, and waiting on God.

In addition to these teachings, we spent a few days before leaving for our "outreach phase" learning how to write and deliver messages and testimonies to different audiences. After returning from outreach we were prepared for re-entry back into "the real world."

The school ran from September 18, 2011 through March 6, 2012. The lecture phase happened two years after all of the unfortunate California memories resurfaced and I was having a hard time again. During this time, I was doing a great amount of wrestling with God in both my mind and heart. I had thought I left it behind in counseling and that I had let go of any lingering memories in Africa. Yet, some of these things had come back as haunting attacks on my faith while I was at YWAM. It wasn't uncommon for my leaders and team members to stop me in the hall to check in. They would often find me and feel the need to stop whatever they were doing to pray with me or enjoy a mug of chicken noodle soup with hot sauce while reviewing our Bible study or class notes. These were the moments that the Lord moved through my classmates to heal me.

I hadn't realized how much bitterness and resentment I had built up over the years after I was raped.

I didn't realize I was mad at God.

I had forgiven the man, but I still blamed God for not intervening.

I was mad at God for not changing the man's actions somehow.

If He was all powerful, and loves me, why didn't He prevent it?

I eventually realized, over soup with a wise friend we all called "Momma", that it was not God's fault that the guy had exercised his free will the way he did. At the end of the day, we are each responsible for our own decisions, which is why it is important to consider the weight of our actions. Not even a month into the school, I was already pushing away the few guys that were there. All they wanted was to be a friend, but I didn't know how to trust them. I knew that they were different, that they weren't doing drugs or looking to take advantage of me. Still, I feared being dominated again and didn't believe that God would protect me. My trust issues caused me to hold all five of my male teammates at arm's length, but I did not stop there.

I pushed God away as well.

Midway through October, I wrote in my journal: *Truth is, with each day, I am getting more and more uncomfortable with the guys. This probably isn't a good thing because I have caught myself using the facial sarcasm and more fake physical and emotional attitudes in this past week around them. We have all been talking more, so it didn't seem like anything was wrong, but I get scenarios in my mind that scare me to death. My rape has been on my mind stronger each time any of them touch me. It could be a simple as a pat on the back or a high-five, but images just leap to the forefront of my memory, even though I know none of them would try anything like that.*

They were like my brothers; why was I freaking out like this? A few nights later, Momma and I were having a heart-to-heart in the lounge. She pointed out that the reason I was shutting down around them was most likely because we were five weeks into the school—the same amount of time that my rapist was my next-door neighbor before he turned on me. I automatically put up walls as a form of self-defense, without consciously realizing it.

That night, I forgave him—again.

Momma and I wrapped up our conversation and headed to bed. On the way back to our dorms, we passed one of the guys in the main hallway. He held out his clenched hand for a fist bump, which seemed fine with me in the moment, so I followed through. He then tried to follow it with a hug. After hesitating for an awkward moment, I turned it down, knowing I could not emotionally handle it. All it was a simple hug from one friend to another. Yet, I struggled to receive casual, appropriate physical touch. I was angry, and my hostility was directed mostly at God but released towards classmates.

A few days later, I received a voicemail from my sister and a matching text from a good high school friend. Both informed me that one of the girls from the 2010 graduating class had died in a car accident. This news left me in shock for several hours, as our school traveled for a week retreat at a nearby lake, unable to feel anything until breaking down some time later after resettling. One of my sweet friends saw me crying during a prayer time and gave me a big hug. Through the tears, I was barely able to tell her what happened.

That night, I sat in bed and journaled about the accident before telling the four other girls who I shared a room with. I knew the friend who died was with Jesus, so I asked them to pray for the girl's family and friends who were left behind to grieve. This gave us a level of peace, even in the midst of questions and confusion. In that moment, I felt like there was every reason to be mad at God for this too; yet, the last words I chose to write in that journal entry simply stated, *I AM NOT MAD AT GOD.*

During the last three months of our DTS, we split up into four teams and went out on mission trips for six weeks. Collectively, we covered most of the globe, then came back to our base and debriefed our experiences before teaming up with a few people from different teams for a two-week "stateside" tour to churches, schools, and youth/home groups. It was incredible to see how people were touched by our stories and testimonies of seeing God work!

My initial overseas outreach had been to Southeast Asia (specifically, Tailand, Burma, and Malaysia) with eleven others (one of whom was just eighteen months old), where we ministered and prayer walked in nine different cities and saw God move in powerful ways. Back in the states, I was placed on a team of eight that ventured into Ohio and Pennsylvania before returning back to the base for graduation.

In Asia, we mainly worked with children who had been rescued out of the sex trafficking trade—girls and boys alike—some as young as three or four years old who had escaped or been rescued. We also spent time with young boys who were rescued from the Burmese army. (By government law, every family must give up one son at age eight to join the army. They seldom see each other again, and when they do, the child is brainwashed by war and rather emotionless.) One little girl we worked with was just two years old when her family began sending her out to chop wood. She wasn't viewed as a prized possession, as a sweet and valuable little girl. Her story, and so many others, tore my heart wide open. They were all so beautiful, in spite of experiencing so much pain and difficulty in their short lives before we met. I would love to adopt any of them, but amongst other hurdles, it is basically impossible because most of them don't have papers or birth certificates. majority of the children living in the orphanage or hill tribes on the Thailand side of the border were smuggled over with fake papers. Normally I am not an advocate of falsified documents, but these ones literally saved lives. Our local contacts explained that some of the children still have parents or other family members who they see now and then over holiday breaks from school. But when they do go home, they just work and often are not treated well or fed regularly. Our teams received extra donations from supporters before leaving the U.S. that were put directly to "spoil the kids" parties.

My team also worked with an organization in southern Thailand that helped people working in one of the biggest red-light tourist scenes (i.e. "sex tourism") on the island of Phuket. When they turn sixteen, many girls come down from the rural north thinking there are endless job opportunities waiting for them in the hospitality industry when they arrive in Phuket. Nine times out of ten, they aren't hired because they don't speak English. To compensate, they usually end up working in bars each evening to make a living and those who hear about opportunities begin taking English classes in the morning. These bar jobs usually start out as a transitional form of income and any money they had left after paying bills was sent home to support the family. There are two types of bars there, "open" and "closed." There is typically one of each right next to each other, tightly packed along side streets off the main road connecting this commercial corner of the island. "Open" bars are open-air and the girls can be bought out by tourists (or locals) for the night. These girls can typically quit work at will. "Closed" bars have a door and walls that you cannot see through from either side. These are considered especially dangerous and notoriously have trafficked, frequently drugged, girls inside being forced to do all sorts of things (the ministry would not further explain to us) while their pimps hang out nearby, keeping a watchful eye on them.

We were only allowed to visit open bars, ordering soda or juice and dressing modestly. Our orders, attire, conversation, and eye contact assured the friends we made, bar girls (or, sometimes, guys) that we were safe and trustworthy people. They often told us that they noted "something different and comfortable" about us, which made conversations easy. It was our spiritual light in the darkness of Bangla Road. Alternating evenings, half of our team went out to befriend employees at whichever bar we felt God was leading us to, while the other half of the team stayed back at the ministry base and prayed for the ones who went out. We were typically out from 9:00 to midnight each night, striking up conversations with the girls who worked at the bars. We would visit some of the bars multiple times during our stay because we wanted to continue investing in those friendships and sharing any resources they may need once they finished school.

At the bars, it is not uncommon to see girls draw men into the bars by dancing on top of the counters. This would often go on for hours, at the instruction of their bosses to drum up business. Some girls would even go out to the streets, grab random men by the hands, and literally pull them over to a bar stool and strike up conversation with whatever English they knew. A select few, normally appearing to be brought in from Russia and drugged, would be showcased like animals in a zoo, standing or dancing spectacles in a small, clear box that was suspended above an intersection where the main road met a side street that were packed with bars. Imagine a bustling street flooded with people of all ages, of different nationalities, most in their 20s to 60s, visiting as tourists from Australia, Western Europe, the U.K., and the States. Many would spend hours searching the hundreds of bars for "the best bar" with "the best girls" in seas of hundreds to rent out for the night.

A typical bar would have six to eight girls working each night, all of whom were "available for hire" but technically "free" to deny a client. I use this term loosely, because their pimps or managers were watching and wanted them to bring in as much money as possible. If a boss or pimp felt a girl didn't bring in enough money, they would threaten to beat them, destroy their passports, or hurt their families. The entire industry runs on intimidation and fear and is fueled by a lust for power and control. The worldwide sex industry is a multi-billion-dollar empire, which tragically continues to increase both in view numbers and sadistic acts with each passing day, based on supply, demand, and the search for love.

We would pass the time in the bars playing games like Jenga while getting to know the employees. We would then invite some of them to meet us outside of work for coffee or a trip to the beach. This was a great opportunity to share with them about the English classes and resources our local ministry friends offered. If the girls were interested, we got their contact information and the organization followed up with them. We knew that those who had the opportunity to learn English would have access to better jobs like waitressing or working at hotels. Some members of our team are still in contact with girls we met on this trip today.

While in Malaysia, we worked with an Indian Tamil-speaking church. There we led Bible studies, shared testimonies, and performed skits. We were of the first YWAM teams to visit this region, which meant we had few local contacts. We spent a lot of time in prayer while walking the neighborhoods near our hotel and the church. One day, we were out praying when two of the girls on our team felt that God was leading them to spend some time cleaning the park near our hotel, which we did on one of our final days there. Another day, we broke into small groups of four and walked the streets to pray. Along the way, one of our groups heard about a massive Hindu festival that takes place on the island of Penang. Attendance reaches 300,000 to 400,000 people each year, a perfect ministry opportunity even with language barriers. Our team prayed about going to minister however we could at the festival and half of us felt God was leading us in this direction, myself included. We felt God was calling us, that His peace would be with us, and He would protect us.

Our team leaders warned us that the spiritual climate would be insanely heavy there and to be praying even before we left our hotel the morning of the festival. As we were in transit, I was asking God to help me document the day as the team photographer. Festival attendees are not spectacles and are deeply valued and loved by Him, the same as anyone else. Still, there is only so much preparation you can do before seeing what we saw that day. The worst of it was witnessing the Hindu men graphically pierce themselves with small and large hooks to show devotion to an idol. The hooks traveled down both sides of their spines and are tethered to another young man who they pull along the festival route. The men do not bleed or scar, as they are demonically possessed the whole time they are pierced. Our whole time there, roughly four hours, we declared God's love out loud over anyone we brushed shoulders with while pressing through the crowd. We spoke Jesus' name with our claimed authority into people who we made eye contact with, and sang any worship song that God sent from our mouths from Chris Tomlin's *God of this City* to songs for the kids running around, such as *Jesus Loves Me*.

The whole time we were there interceding, I took 750 photos on my camera. Reviewing them later on, I counted only five people who were smiling. Everyone else looked so empty, lost, confused, and restless. You could see it in their eyes. Even now, I so want to go back and invite more of them to encounter the true Father right there, despite the massive chaos. As forewarned, the experience God led us through at the festival took a huge toll on those of us who went. We believe we were being attacked spiritually through our physical and mental health the next few days. Personally, I was attacked, even terrorized, and couldn't even speak about it with anyone who wasn't there for three to four weeks after attending and returning home. Neither my mind nor my tongue was able to process or form the words needed to speak up about everything that went on there. When we returned to Wisconsin to debrief our experience, we were asked about this day and my mind shut down as I stared at the floor, tearing up, while someone else shared. Those will remain as stories for another time. Luckily for all of us, God is faithful and helped me pull through so I was better able to share other stories on stateside tours.

We saw some crazy stuff and experienced so much spiritual warfare while we were over on the other side of the world. Many of the teams had a challenging time to process much of the trips, respectively, for a few months after coming back to the States. However, in all of this, God showed me so much of His overflowing grace and overwhelming adoration that He has in stock for each moment. The Lord is so faithful.

One night, between graduation and a financial seminar, a few of us went to our base leader's house for a fun game night. I was sitting in the corner just thinking "grand scheme" level with God as I looked around at some of the people in the room. In that moment, it was as though God allowed me to see partial flashback videos of their lives, the hard moments they have experienced. I saw one girl crying on the floor, cornered, being yelled at by her dad. I saw another girl walk in on her sister doing drugs when they were supposed to go out and spend time together. Another was being physically abused. Two more were running, separately, in search of attention, love, and value. One guy was tired of doing all of the "right" things; another was done doing all of the "wrong" things. Some of us come from a history where our clothes were stripped from us, along with our innocence. Some of us come from a place where it is unheard of to wake up with bruises that you know are not from simply wrestling with your brothers.

I was talking with another sweet DTS friend's dad the day after our graduation, a week earlier, and do you know what he told me?

He said, "I am glad that we have these four minutes to talk right now because I have one thing I want you to hear: Thank you for being my daughter's friend and investing in her life. You have had a huge impact on her over the past few months, whether you realize it or not. Helping her heal and process the past number of years and with the uncertainty of life's end, time is so precious. Too precious not to heal and walk freely."

Returning to Denver after experiencing all that was tough. It was different from the two prior trips to Africa. Finding a new normal while processing that kind of whirlwind was more challenging than initially saying "yes" to the unknown of exploring more life outside of Colorado. When I left for the school, I left friendships at home on pause. I didn't fully realize then that those wonderful people would continue to grow and change in their own ways, while I did the same 965 miles away in Wisconsin and beyond. Not only was it like this for friendships in those six months, but every time I left for mission trips.

Chapter 6

FRIENDSHIPS AND MOVING TO A WAR ZONE

One day after church, one of my best friends and I went to lunch and the topic of friendship came up. I could tell she wasn't quite herself that day. As she spoke, she told me what was on her mind. She said that she had noticed every time I left Denver, the dynamic between my friends and I would drastically change. More often than not, they felt abandoned, like they got the short straw and felt as though I cared more about strangers than about them.

"You're going off every few months to go change the world and we're still here just living life, which goes on while you're gone. Things are always different when you come back. So, in that way, you cannot expect everyone to be super excited to see you when you come home. We have to mentally prepare to spend more of life without you."

I was not aware that there seemed to be this expectation coming from me, so this conversation was both blindsiding and good to have. Obviously, it was fun when they got excited that I would be in town and reminded me that I am loved here, too. My friend told me that she had found herself withdrawing a bit from our friendship. But she also mentioned that she really doesn't want to get too emotionally invested in our relationship, because "who knows when you'll be back for good or take off again." Maybe it is a lot to expect from someone. She said she knows that what I'm doing is important but that doesn't change the fact that she misses her best friend when I am out exploring new places.

I understand it is difficult to be the friend of a missionary. I'm the one who gets to go on amazing adventures in new places, collecting stories to share while my friend is back at home in school or working, missing me and perhaps growing a bit jealous. Sure, she loves and supports me, but that doesn't change the fact that she would rather be somewhere else as well. I guess it is a difficult mixture of emotions to swallow. After we had this chat, I was glad we talked but was also honestly hurt. All I could think in response was, *does this mean she doesn't like to cherish precious time and make every second we do have in the same city count? Am I not worth a few more months of devoted friendship and mutual encouragement? She could be traveling too...*

There are many reasons why I try to spend as much time as possible investing in friends while I am home. I want to show them that I've missed them and that they do matter to me. For instance, Laurene and I used to enjoy going to the bookstore and drinking coffee or hot chocolate while reading comics to each other. I cherish the day another friend and I had a picnic in the park with juice boxes like little kids just before we both turned 21. Another memory was from spending an entire day "wasting" gas driving through the Rocky Mountains on a photoshoot day with another good friend. With all my friends from home, I value our time together when we are able to have it. Catching up with my friends and hearing about what has been taking place in their lives is one of my favorite ways to pass the time. I treasure these moments before I leave for a new trip, and look forward to them when I return to Colorado. While I understand the feeling of being left behind, I enjoy being able to catch up with my friends when I come back home.

Being in full-time missions, I think there is a fine line between expecting people to want to hear your stories and expecting people to be automatically closed off to them. It's been said that while you are at home, you get comfortable in your routine. Missions life is quite the opposite, being all about flexibility. For example, back when I worked full-time as a barista at a coffee shop in 2009, I had a very set routine. Since it was the coffee business, obviously, most days began quite early. Every morning was predictable and routines were set. My reason for so much cardio was that the following spring I was planning on auditioning with a local theater company for a stage show of *Chicago*. The show was rumored to have intense dance routines. Anyone who does much theater work knows that between dance and vocals, you have to be in great shape to keep up. I picked up running as a pastime and ran at least an hour each day, minimum five days a week, through downtown Littleton. It was just a matter of if I had enough energy to go before passing out versus waiting for the weather to cool off a bit first. In Colorado, running outside almost daily from the middle of May through August is one of the best ways to get fresh air, which is especially nice when your apartment stairwell often smells like marijuana. Since this season, I have had a bad track record of really getting into running and working out, especially when a change in scenery keeps me from sticking with it. When I had moved to Lake Tahoe for ski season it wasn't practical to keep running, picked it up with classmates in Madison, then lost it again later on as it wasn't necessarily encouraged or safe to go running in Mexico—either by myself or with other staff. Running indoors on a machine was often the best solution, but that would leave me feeling encaged.

Back to friendships in 2012. One spring evening, I was catching up out with another of my best friends. She told me that she knows her life isn't pleasing God, and that some of the things she's involved in hurt her as well. Hearing this made me so sad, because I wanted the best for her but I didn't know how to put what I thought that advice was into words. I tried to remind her how much God has done for her and how He much He still loves her. It was the truth, but it sounded a bit cheesy when I said it out loud.

In this and other situations, I feel like I'm always "that friend" who is always talking about God, how awesome He is, and how I want to follow His plan for my life rather than my own plans. I can hear the devil whispering lies in my ears as I say those things, he says divisive things like, *Stop talking! The person to your left thinks you are crazy right now. Your friends don't care about people who are trafficked out of Russia and forced into prostitution; if they did, they would go help them themselves.*

In those moments, my response is often along the lines of, *if they didn't care, why did THEY ask me for stories and pictures of Asia? Why did THEY initiate this meeting over coffee? They do care.* Raising awareness of injustice is a constant battle. A classmate from DTS worded it perfectly in a note she put online shortly after our graduation: "[Christian missionary life] has made it far more difficult for us to just blend in, to just go with the flow. We were meant to be different and stand out. We are not of this world and that realization really hit when we left school. We have grown closer to God on a far more intimate level than anything we have known before. This means we are in tune with His heart and His thoughts. We asked to see people the way He sees them. We asked to see the world how He sees it. We asked to be broken by what breaks His heart. He answered our prayers and yet we are confused as to why re-entry is so difficult?"

My heart hurt for my friend, especially that she changed so much while I was gone and I still struggled to understand why. I was only away for a few months! But then I remember, I'm a different person than I was when I left, too. I don't regret leaving because I love when God allows me to see what He sees, feel what He feels, or cry when He cries. I asked for these things, and He answers prayers.

My friends here at home often ask me why I leave all the time, what am I trying to hide from here. Without instantly having an emotional breakdown on them, I try to kindly respond something along the lines of mentioning that there are presently 47,000,000 orphans on the other end of my driveway. I know I cannot love each of them, but that won't stop me from loving some on each trip I go on. Or maybe it's because I recently learned that little boys in Burma are forced into the army and adults in South Africa are selling their babies to be raped by their neighbors in order to afford to buy a little bit of contaminated water or have drug money. I am simply being a conduit for God's work in the here and now, as He cares for all of these needs and desires to meet them through His people. I'm able and willing to say "yes" and step out.

Goodbyes are never easy. It's hard to get attached, to get comfortable with your family and friends, and then have to—or choose to—leave. It's tough being always on the go, constantly leaving those that you're so close and familiar with. But that's part of missions; it's part of the surrender and sacrifice that we give to the Lord. We allow Him to move us where He wants us, to be His hands and feet.

There is nothing quite as sweet as the thin mountain air of the *mile high city*, but I have tasted the air of adventure, the oxygen in foreign countries. The more of that I taste, the more I desire. I love traveling to new cities, meeting new people, and experiencing new cultures. Hearing about people who live their entire lives in a ten-block radius breaks my heart. God created so much more for us to experience with our senses. We shouldn't live in fear of what bad things *could* happen should we adventure a bit. Rather, we should travel with wisdom.

Within a few weeks being home from Wisconsin, routine

settled in again. This included diving back into those sweet worship nights at the home of some dear friends. Within a month of being back, I felt the Lord invite me to begin writing this book you are now holding.

The backstory is best explained through a conversation He and I had one evening in worship.

Ellie, do you realize how I've helped you through so many detrimental events throughout your life? I felt God ask, even mentioning a few specific examples.

Yes, definitely! Thank you, yet again.

Great! Well, of course, My daughter, where else would I have been in those times? Now we are going to write about it all! Anticipating my response, *But don't worry, I'll help you with this as well.*

Um, okay! I said, hesitating a bit. Little did I realize in that moment the full implications. This would be the ultimate vulnerability with everyone who touches this book from the beginning to end, until forever.

Awesome! With this book of your testimony, people will be able to see My faithfulness and know that hope is real! They'll understand Me a little bit more after reflecting on all I've seen you through and possibly be more open for Me in their own lives.

As the summer of 2012 begun, I worked as a nanny for a family with three youngsters. I was able to explain the Gospel to these littles by the end of summer. I found myself becoming bolder and brighter when it came to sharing the good news of Christ with others.

For me, even with further discipleship and evangelism training, I have learned that it's never quite comfy to step out in faith for the Lord. But in trusting God, you can allow Him to work through you the way He needs to in order to impact another life. Allowing the Lord to fill your mouth with words when you speak can be frightening—no matter the size of your audience—but it will skyrocket your level of trust in Him and who He is. Had I kept track of every conversation I've had with strangers due to feeling a nudge from the Holy Spirit, whether it went well or not, I could fill another book. These moments often begin timidly, with stuttering, risking looking a complete fool. And you know what? Those conversations often end up being the most fun! It is a matter of knowing who you are and calling out who someone else is so their heart is awakened to purpose.

That whole summer, I was seeking to raise monthly support for my upcoming long term YWAM commitment to minister on the El Paso, Texas/Juárez, Mexico border—primarily in the children's home on the ministry base, south of the border. Simultaneously, and for six years previously, there was (put lightly) a lot of violence in this city where the Lord asked me to go. When the opportunity came about, the conversation was brief. He promised "Within a year, I'll have you living in Mexico and volunteering in a children's home in Juárez."

I responded, "Umm, I was really hoping to get back to Africa again soon, can that happen instead?" He so gently said "Later, I'll bring you back there for a bit later. But first, we hit the Borderland."

Finding financial, much less prayer support, was a battle wherever I turned. Most of my friends responded in fear for my life and would not support the move and spoke negativity over it instead. Aside from an appeal letter I wrote, prayed over, and sent out with little response, many conversations went something like this:

Me: "I feel like God clearly told me He wants me to move to Juárez for two years to serve at the YWAM missions base. I have not been there specifically before, but spent a week outside the city on a trip volunteering elsewhere during high school, and now feel led to primarily help out at the children's home this base operates. Would you prayerfully consider giving some form of monthly support to help me accomplish this?"

Almost Everyone: "Do you know what has been happening in Juárez? Do you even watch the news?!" (Interestingly enough, both Christians and non-Christians would often respond in this manner.)

Me: "No, I'm only twenty-two; I don't watch the news. What's going on?"

Almost Everyone: "Femicide. Genocide. Drugs. Cartels. Most churches have stopped sending teams down there to build homes because it's so dangerous!"

Me: "Huh, you don't say? Well … it makes sense why God wants me to go there then!"

Almost Everyone: "You're really going to go?"

Me: "I mean, He said to go and we all saw what happened to Jonah in the Bible when he disobeyed the Lord's leading. I am totally confident that I'll come back alive after my commitment is up, but even if I don't, God is worthy of my obedience."

Almost Everyone: "Wow. Okay, well, I agree, but I also think you are crazy and will most likely die—or should be aware that you could be kidnapped by the cartel or a gang, raped repeatedly, and held for ransom from the American Church because you are a beautiful, white, female missionary. Hope it all works out and we'll see you in Heaven if you don't make it back home!"

Me: "So, to clarify … you will not be supporting me financially then?"

This is no joke or exaggeration as to what occurred. This is the opposition the enemy was throwing at me time and time again as I tried harder and harder to respond in obedience to the Lord, and these conversations sparked my spirit to head down to the border as soon as possible. Trusting the Lord's timing and provision in this way was not easy. Nevertheless, I had no reservations or fear about moving. I knew in my heart what the Lord was calling me to do, but I did have some weird dreams that summer.

One week that July, I woke up from a dream where I was kidnapped in Colorado, thrown in the trunk of a vehicle, and taken south on the interstate toward the Mexican border. At a rest stop, the four men were shooting up with needles and had a toy gun that was like a Pez dispenser and "shot" little, colorful, circular, quickly dissolving pills—illegal drugs. As they were each getting high with mixes of syringes and these pills, the leader grabbed me and "shot" one of the pills into my mouth. I pretended to receive it, being the hostage, but as soon as he let go, I spit it at him, kicked him in the face, and ran. Somehow, despite their state of mind, they managed to catch up to me.

Dreams are funny things, because after that scene I was also part of the search and rescue party that was sent out to find me. We searched all over the mountainside of Colorado Springs and the surrounding area before I woke up. This dream was interpreted by a couple of the elders from my church. Through a lot of prayer and insight, they called me a few days later and said they felt this was not just a nightmare as much as it was encouragement from God that I needed to keep pressing forward.

A week later, I had a short dream that was just a repeating image, like a GIF. It was of a person standing in a massive, white space and there was a sword that slashed the person across the abdomen, causing their organs to burst forth with water and blood. This would graphically reoccur over and over until I woke up in a panic.

This was also the summer of the tragic Aurora theater shooting, which was not more than half an hour from my home. Several of my friends almost attended a showing at that exact theater that night, but decided not to at the last minute. A few days after the shooting, I was on the phone with a member of the YWAM El Paso-Juárez staff, explaining about the opposition with getting people to pledge monthly support. He said, "I do not want to offend your family or friends, but if nobody in Colorado can safely see a movie in the theater, your state is no different than this city."

A few weeks later, after some close friends and I returned from a weekend conference in Los Angeles, a number of people asked, "Hey, aren't you about to move to the local war zone?"

Each time I responded, "Yes, soon! I'm trying to raise monthly support in order to get established down there." I had a goal to move by mid-September, just a random date

I was telling people for a while so they knew plans were in motion. After having several of these conversations back to back, I was driving home when I realized that if it was God who said I should move down there, then He should choose the date and make it happen. I knew He would take care of all the details, and I was done trying to orchestrate it all myself, so I handed it over to him then and there. Before I had even finished that prayer, my phone rang. It was the staffer calling to ask if I was available to move at the end of the following week! (It goes to show that God operates on His own schedule.) The conversation after we exchanged pleasantries was pretty brief.

"We were wondering if you are able to move here at any point on the weekend of the seventeenth?"

"A week from this Friday?" I confirmed.

"Yeah, if it works. Another family will be getting here at the same time so we can get you all through orientation together, and then you can attend our staff retreat with us and dive into the ministry from there." He was so casual, making this seem completely doable.

"Okay, I'll check airfare once I get home and get back to you."

I got home and told my mom what happened. Within an hour, I was on the phone with him again, letting him know the details of a last minute, one-way flight we had found for under $200!

Needless to say, it was an insane ten days of getting everything together to move to what was one of the "top ten most dangerous cities in the world" at the time. To this day, when I think back, it's such a blur but the most notable event between all of the goodbyes was being prayed over at that final worship night. The guy who normally led these worship nights got an incredibly Holy Spirit-inspired prophetic song. He felt the Lord told him to record the song on my phone so I could take it with me and play it over the kids (and myself) whenever we needed encouragement, refreshment, or reminders of God's nearness. Years later, it still gives me chills.

May there be a new song on my lips
May I not be triumphed in this desert storm
As the rain falls from Your kiss upon my forehead

And I know that You will be with me
When all of the walls come crashing down
I'll look to the ground and find the little one You love
and draw them in my arms as You have drawn me

And may I fall more in love with You
As I touch a heart that never knew
That a love so great would call for me
I release it over all, over all that they may see
Your love shining bright
A love like the stars in the night
May they see Your love shining bright, like the stars that
    burn in the night

There's a fire that's deep in my heart
No one here on Earth could ever put this fire out
Cause Your love for me can never be quenched
Your love is my life
And my identity is found in being with You

Nothing can separate me from Your great love
Or the riches You have for me
Cause You have spilled Your precious blood
And broken the seal of death over me
You've broken the seal of death over me
You've broken the seal of death over me
You've broken the seal.
I will rise and thank the Lord
Oh how I'll sing of what He has done for me
All of the nations will rejoice when they see a King who
     has slid the ring on His bride's hand
The ring on His bride's hand, Your love for me
Mmm oh, Your love for me

And I know that soon I will be with You forever
I know that soon I will be home with the Love that's never
     left me alone
I know that soon I will be with You forever
I know that soon I will be we will home, I will not be alone

'Cause my Jesus He loves me
That's the song and the theme that is above me
The banner on my heart—He's written upon my heart
And I'll sing
Yes my Jesus He loves me
That's the banner that's over me
He's the banner above my heart – He's written it on my heart

My Jesus He loves me so
He loves me so.

This song got me through many rough days in the Mexican desert. Never will I say again that Jesus does not know me or understand what intense feelings of all sorts of loneliness are like, because He is the very one who *designed* emotion. For me, the lyrics in the first two stanzas alone speak volumes to my heart. Specifically, *May I not be triumphed in this desert storm / As the rain falls from Your kiss upon my forehead / And I know that You will be with me / When all of the walls come crashing down* attests to just that. Jesus woos us when He addresses our hearts. He understands and is always faithful to tend to every one of our needs if we allow Him to do so. Also, He knows I love rain.

I could go stanza by stanza and explain what it all means to me personally, but instead I'll allow you to receive your own interpretation and connections if you would like, as I know God can speak to multiple people through the same words in a totally unique way.

I will address one more line, because it is crucial for the time and place of the song and move.

Cause You have spilled Your precious blood / And broken the seal of death over me.

Juárez was riddled with blood and death for years before I moved in. Once I arrived, I saw empty streets and a general feeling of utter hopelessness over the damaged and grieving city. Jesus died once for all on the cross, shedding His blood so nobody else would ever have to. This is the Gospel story and it is truly life-changing. He took me there to bring hope back to the Borderland, as part of a resident team who (along with other local churches and relief groups) were weary of the fighting. Anyone could have done what I did but God told me part of the plan and I responded, "I will go." Within a month before my move to the city, the daily death tolls began to subside. As I understand it, one of the main cartels died out, and the Feds quickly cleared any others. The Lord is a God of miracles; here we now are with these testimonies in hand.

I lived at, or near, the YWAM base on the south side of the border from August 17, 2012 to October 23, 2014. Being "on staff" with YWAM essentially means being a full-time volunteer. No one, not even the original creators of the organization or base directors, receives a salary from YWAM, but instead raises their own financial support and prayer covering through friends and family.

Before, during, and after becoming a YWAM-er I spent a lot of time sharing my heart with family and friends, inviting them to sow into the vision and future of the place I was going. Through my relational network, a handful of people chose to support me financially, either with one-time gifts or a set amount each month.

Communication and relationship are both huge values. Traveling so much, newsletters and Facebook posts ended up as my main form of communication with family and friends, with the occasional appeal letter and phone call. This was a different endeavor from any other trip I had been on before. What I mean by that is, past trips required me to raise a smaller (while still significant) amount of money, one-time, and then I was done. Living on the mission field, however, required monthly support to sustain. The amount varies from base to base, family to family, and person to person. It is dependent upon their budget, whether or not they are married or single, and how many kids they may have (if any). It also depends on what part of the world they are called to, as the cost of living can vary dramatically. With this base, donations are processed in the U.S. and being a resident of the States, I was still responsible to pay taxes on income—even as a full-time volunteer. For this particular base, an individual would ideally need to raise between $700 to $1,000 in monthly support.

I was extremely underfunded throughout, despite all my efforts, which was not ideal. Typically, between my four consistent supporters and others who gave when they could, I received just under $400 each month. As funds came in, I would immediately write a thank you note and direct the first allotment for my rent and staff fees (which covered the costs of maintaining the aspects of the base we all shared), *then* budget for anything else I needed personally so I could stay as much out of debt to the ministry as possible. There were a few times when I did fall behind on my room and board, especially when I would attempt to simultaneously raise funds for separate ministry trips, courses, or apply for Mexican residency. In all of this, I found that God always provided at least enough and His grace was sufficient for me in the in-between moments. I can honestly tell you it was fun, even if stressful at times, to see how the Lord chose to provide over the years. There were times when unexpected checks would show up in the mail. Sometimes, there were notes designating the surprise gift toward my expenses or a ministry trip; other times, there would simply be a note attached that said, "We miss you; go have some fun!"

For these two years, I lived without a car to call my own. While this helped keep my cost of living extra low, those who know me can tell you this was one of my greatest challenges because I enjoy the sense of freedom and adventure that owning a car brings. (For me, driving with loud music and unrolled windows is a major stress reliever.) Luckily, the base had a few cars we were able to use when we needed them, and I had friends who would either bring me on errands with them or loan me their cars to take into town or across to Texas for the afternoon to gather supplies or run errands. In lieu of driving at will, another good stress relieving method a dear friend and I found there was to run around in thunderstorms. We jumped, laughed, danced, sung, and screamed puddle to puddle in as many torrential downpours and floods as we could. Granted, anytime it stormed enough for a good time, the roads in our neighborhood were all torn up and many houses flooded, so us playing in rain was really trying to make the best of bad situations.

Just as important as financial support, and maybe even more important, is having a team of people who support you through prayer. This is truly critical. The first few things that come to mind now, more than a year after returning to Colorado, are the times when friends from home would text me while I was in Mexico. They would say things like, *God just brought you to mind and I miss you so much today! How can I best be praying for you?* Being remembered by someone back home when I was off on my own would usually bring me to tears. A sweet and simple text or voicemail can encourage somebody and change their entire week, and it only takes a few moments of one's day to be the sender of this form of encouragement. If you have friends or acquaintances in "the field," either locally or overseas, I encourage you to go get ahold of them and encourage them in some way. If they cannot be reached at all, just commit to pray for them and trust the Lord to give them the comfort and peace they may need. I can assure you that even short prayers are powerful!

During the twenty-six months I lived in Mexico, I primarily ministered at the children's home. The directors of the home oversaw and supported the rest of the staff (i.e. disciplinary backup for the youths when time outs were not enough) as we worked half or full-day shifts with the kids, teens, and pre-teens. We were usually short-handed, and there were about forty kids, so we definitely had good days and bad days. As time went on, there were many issues that arose, particularly involving those who came from distressed and broken homes. Being that they were raised with less than ideal values, before coming to us and being introduced to Jesus Christ, they would often react to our instruction and leadership by yelling hateful words at us. This was hard for me to deal with, given my background but I realized it was all they knew as a way to express most feelings. Over time, we developed better ways of understanding the older kids and helped them learn to express their emotions in more healthy ways. Building trust then relationship was especially challenging with this age group, and also the most vital factor to being successful as a voice permitted to speak into their lives. My whole first year of consistency, patience, healthy and respectful distance did wonders to lay that basis of trust with many of the youth. Once they learned I am a safe person who isn't about to take off, they finally began to slowly open up. Early on in my second year, one of the highest compliments I received from one of the thirteen-year-old boys was one evening when he came up to me and asked "Miss, may I call you *Mom*?"

Honored beyond words with the warmest heart and near tears, I had to remind him the rules say that is not allowed for the bond it creates and can lead to jealousy between children.

With the little children, we did things differently. With them, their hurt was not in process yet, mostly stored away in their memories to sort through later. Besides being innocently sworn at by a three-year-old girl one time, I received more snuggles and hugs from this age group during my commitment. Aside from nightly devotionals before lights out, tucking them in, and praying with them each night before leaving them to sleep listening to worship music, there were two especially noteworthy moments that have stuck with me. Once, early on, there was an evening that held an extra bedtime story that two of the pre-adolescents asked for shortly after I began working there, which I let God tell through me because I didn't know enough Spanish. The other moment took place when the kids were coloring. It was simple enough, but as I watched one of the boys color in a super hero coloring book, I nearly cried. Instead of sulking at the table while he missed the movie for detention, he was flying through the skies and fighting crime! Coloring can be a great therapy and a healthy escape from reality.

Aside from the home, I helped create and co-lead a "red light outreach" with three other women who primarily staffed in other departments of the ministry. We have similar hearts in relation to the sex industry—a desire to see justice prevail, vulnerable women no longer taken advantage of, and men set free from the chains of lust and control. I enjoyed being a part of these prayer times and regular outreaches, and the other women continue this ministry to this day along with others who have since joined the team. Even though I am no longer actively serving in this ministry in Mexico, it is still very close to my heart.

The entire base staff was invited to intercede for this branch of the ministry, especially for specific individuals who are caught up in the industry and crossed our paths. We also opened it up to anyone on the base to join us on what we called Block Party outreaches. These were targeted outreaches where our teams would spend an extra night out on the streets, inviting God's presence to fill the downtown area where many seedy activities take place after dark. As we went from street to street, we invited God to shift the atmosphere and invited women who were working out of different motels to attend the free party we were hosting just for them. They would be treated to dinner, coffee, manicures, and basically just to be rightly adored! The block parties were such a great outreach to these women because they gave them the chance to feel loved and valued in an appropriate and empowering manner. We wished we were able to do these events more often, but due to the cost of putting them on the team is only able to do once or twice each year.

Men and women, who "willingly" work in the sex industry selling their own bodies in return for drugs or money, are commonly referred to as *prostitutes*, a term that usually carries a negative sentiment with most people. However, the prostituted women that I have come to know through global outreach are some of the sweetest and most protective people. They are rowdy, because they like to have a good time and still enjoy life, but this does not fully define who they are. And, to be honest, they aren't that much different from you and me—they like to have a good time, meaning they have certain interests and preferences. One of the women we met in Juárez told us she wanted to go out dancing with us, even after we all agreed that none of us—herself included—knew how to dance well. She's the type of woman who loves to live in the moment and go with the flow, just so long as it leads to an adventure!

I will say that many of the men and women we met on the streets partake of drugs on some level, but this is primarily only because they feel like they have to do something to cope with the lives they lead; they need an escape of some sort, and candidly shared with us that this was the best option. While you and I may choose to go on a long walk or movie marathon to "escape" from society, they cannot because their reputation precedes them. This doesn't just happen in Mexico but all around the world. They have come to carry themselves in a certain way and face stereotypes everywhere they go, often being treated as "less than" and judged by their appearance. They carry a huge amount of shame related to their profession. So, they turn to drugs to numb the pain and escape from what their lives have become. I don't condone their lifestyles, but I better understand it. This sentiment has only increased as I do more research and personally interact with men and women who have fallen into this deceptively alluring industry.

One of our friends was caught in possession and ended up in jail for a while, then spent several months in rehab until shortly after I returned to the States. We later learned that she is (sadly) now working from a different motel.

As our friendships developed, the girls began to ask us questions about our own lives. They would ask if we have boyfriends, or husbands, or children, and they were continually surprised when each of us responded, "Nope, not yet!" There would be times when their jaws would literally drop. From time to time we would even be asked if we were straight-up nuns, to which we would laugh and explain that we were not, and were "allowed" to date.

Since our first visit, they knew we are Christians. However, we soon found there were many occasions where they had seen Christ misrepresented: be it their initial rapist, their "Johns" (customers), or a coworker. Many people claim to be a "follower of Christ" but not everyone actually lives it out.

There were times when we would be conversing with some of the girls on the streets outside of their motels and a man would approach *us* to inquire for a room. The girls always shooed them off before we could comprehend what happened! When men walk down the street and slow down outside, they glance up and down at every female who is present. When a man's eyes slowed on one of us, the girl we were conversing with would stop mid-conversation, look him in the eye, and say point-blank, "She does not work here; leave her alone." Sometimes, they would say, "They are our friends and come visit us every week because they're nice. They sometimes bring us treats or paint our nails … I told you they don't work here!" Colorful choice words were often included in these confrontations, which I only picked up on because I know I didn't learn those words in Spanish class. The girls knew we did not come to draw away their business, we assured them that was the *last* thing we would do (so, never).

It is like a thousand needles to the heart every time you are mid-conversation with a girl and a man approaches to strike a deal. Before you know it, she turns to you and says, "I'll be back in fifteen minutes; we can keep talking if you're still here."

These women are tough. They will run their mouths at men and at one another, as it is a constant competition of who visits the back rooms most. Most of the women we knew over time through being friends and regular ministry shared with us that they generally make the USD equivalent of roughly $6-8 per client over the course of five to ten hour-long shifts, which vary depending on the day of the week and the weather. The number one alternative job most of these women could do, if they left this industry, is work in local factories. The pay is drastically less, which is mainly what keeps them where they are—surrounded by their abusers. They struggle to pay rent and to support their children, parents, boyfriends, and husbands. One friend in particular shared with us that each day she goes home to her husband. He sometimes greets her, but then always asks how many clients she had that day, then demands all her income… essentially pimping her. Although poverty is rampant in many parts of the developing country, I have noticed that the cost of living is not much different from the States. While rent and seeing a movie at the cinema is generally cheaper, food in many cities is often only a dollar or two different if at all.

One night, our team of four women decided to go on a prayer walk downtown. Looking back, it probably wasn't the wisest choice. As we walked, I thought back to the words my friends had said right before I left Colorado. They had said, "Be careful down there in Juárez," and "Watch your back, Ellie, be smart and safe." Even, "Keep running after Jesus; He's got you tight!"

If only they could see me walking *these* streets with such strong women, following what God had put on my heart and dreaming for more. I wasn't afraid of the city, but most from back home would have slapped me upside the head and drug me back to Denver as fast as they could.

In addition to the children's home and "red light" ministry, I served as an assistant to the base director. There would be days when she would hand me her keys and a list of errands she needed me to run in El Paso, and other days I would make calls and return emails. I helped keep the office up and running, and also served on the intercession, creative arts, and traveling banquet fundraising teams. From time to time, I would also help out when short-term teams visited the base. From hospitality and cleaning up after meals to translating on local outreaches, and for a while aided in the children's school on the base, and weekend outreaches to kids from the neighborhood, I was involved in many different areas of the full ministry. It felt like I did a little bit of everything on the base. If I saw something that needed to be done, I wanted (and felt some pressure be it from myself or others) to be one of the first to volunteer to meet the need. It got to the point where leadership advised me to guard my days off, and taught me that it was okay to say, "I'm sorry; I can't help with that." Ministry burnout is real, and I am grateful for my leaders who helped me make responsible decisions. It can be challenging for me to say "no" without a real reason to back it up, as I tend to be a "people-pleaser" type and genuinely enjoy helping.

In November of 2013 God gave me that chance to go back to Africa, and I of course leaped at the opportunity. Although it was a short-term trip of roughly two weeks minus travel days, I wasn't about to pass up a chance to visit Pemba, Mozambique. Bonus: some close friends from home were able to come, too! The trip was to volunteer in a multitude of ways with Iris Global. Going on a mission trip from the mission field felt funny, but was natural. The ministry there operates a children's home nearly four times the size of the one I was at in Juárez, village feeding program, schools for the youth, ministry and Bible schools, widow outreach, prison ministry, "bush bush" (remote village) evangelism outreaches, just to name some of what they do. Highlights of the week and a half there definitely were village feeding, having the opportunity to go on two separate bush bush trips, and what God did in my heart there.

Village feeding is every afternoon. Many of the neighborhood children (at least one hundred) fill an outdoor chapel at the ministry base where they are told about Jesus and fed what is often their only meal of the day, white rice and pinto beans. This time of day was impactful because of their gleeful giggles and heart filled worship, always super sweet. Bush bush outreach was a totally different experience. Essentially, it is an overnight camping trip sharing the Jesus film in the main tribal language, power evangelism (words of knowledge, healing, and deliverance), home visits, meeting village chiefs and queens, and free medical relief. My favorite bush bush story is from the first outreach while the medical team was there. Men, women and children waited in line for hours to be seen. While waiting, we painted the women and girls' nails. There was an array of polish colors, but we saw something awesome with one in particular: a dark, royal purple which lasted for hours longer than your average bottle of polish. Any time it started to gunk up or dry out from the heat, we just asked God for more! It sounds so simple—because it is! We closed the polish bottle, shook it, and prayed "More Lord!" then opened it and found it good as new; even later in the evening and the following night it was still applying! Seeing God provide small things for us like nail polish reminded the team just how much He adores people! Back at the base, there was one especially notable encounter the Lord brought me into that stood out from the others. I may never have words to quite convey what happened in that time, but oh was it sweet! It began one evening when the base leader shared dinner with our team on the beach and stood up to share a word. By the time he finished, most of the team had fallen slain in the Holy Spirit—endless laughter, tears, you name it. This didn't hit me till later in the evening, but once it did there was no moving. I tried—other teammates who were afraid I'd fall tried—He had me glued by glory in one specific spot, laying on my right side near a ledge. This lasted forty-five minutes and I was hearing everything going on around me in the physical realm, as well as taken somewhere with the Lord in the spiritual. If you have not experienced anything like this, I know it sounds wild and crazy, but take my word for it: it is incredible, and often leaves one speechless. All I know for sure is God was doing really good things deep in my heart during that time. The entire time I was laying there; I was weeping. Any type of crying has felt stifled for me since about 2008, so this release was a huge deal for my heart! I hoped to return to this ministry base long term after finishing my commitment in Mexico, but still haven't made it back to Africa yet.

While in Mexico, I was also able to participate in a month-long immersion YWAM language school, a one-week "Celebrating Children Workshop" with LOOM International, a five-month advanced YWAM Bible course, and a few outreaches.

The language school was mentally intense. We would begin classes at breakfast and go until dinner, the day filled with lessons and activities and homework after hours. Having chosen Spanish as an elective throughout high school, I was able to work with the children who were not bilingual and be in an advanced class. There were several late nights and tears of confusion and frustration from a handful (if not all) of us students... Once I was able to take in everything I was learning, my understanding of the Spanish language increased, as did my connections with the children in the home and the women downtown.

The Celebrating Children Workshop taught participants about the development of the human brain from infancy, as well as the various methods people use to deal with trauma at different ages. One thing that stood out to me most was the concept that it takes ten affirming words to cancel out one negative word spoken to a child. I found this very helpful as I worked with the youngsters at the home, especially with what I knew of many of their backgrounds and the rough spots in their pasts. From that moment on, it made it easier to show them all an extra amount of grace, kindness, and understanding.

The Bible course consisted of a quick yet deep survey of both the Old and New Testaments, and the outreaches we did all over the country were very powerful (to say the least). Before we left on the first outreach to teach in the mountains of central Mexico, each of the team members prayed and ask God which topics from a pre-outlined seminar they should develop and teach at all of the locations we would visit. The two I decided on were entitled *father heart of God* and *consequences of sin*. As you have seen throughout this book, my life experiences lent to many first-hand accounts of things God had taught me in both areas. Though others on the team argued that I could do all of my prep and teaching in Spanish, I ended up teaching on these topics in English and was translated phrase by phrase by a team leader or other bilingual classmate so that everyone could understand and I would not be too afraid of messing up words.

During my last month in Mexico, I transitioned back from learning in the Bible course to my regular assignment working in the children's home. This, however, did not go as smoothly as anticipated. While I had been temporarily relieved from my shifts at the home to focus on my participation in the school, some of the kids who knew me had taken it personally, as though I had suddenly woken up one day and stopped caring for them. When I returned to spend my days with them these thoughts may have been dispelled—until one day when I told them my time in Mexico was ending and I would soon be returning home to Colorado. From that day on, all credibility and rapport I had built and maintained with the older kids over the past two years began to crumble.

"Oh, of course. Another staff is leaving," I heard some say. They were so used to saying good-bye that they no longer tried to hide the attitudes that stemmed from feelings of abandonment. Because of this, I no longer try to call or visit. It hurts, but sometimes a clean break is better for everyone. I would so love to see and hug them all again—the ones who are still there, the ones who have been reunited with their parents, the ones who have since been adopted, the funny ones, the ones who loved to snuggle during weekend movie times, even the more difficult ones. Leaving each of them, the friends downtown, and the few staff members I'd grown close to wasn't easy, but I knew I was faithfully following the next step of God's plan. It was time to come home and write. There was a grace for the transition. Looking back, I'm grateful that I was obedient, but I also realize that leaving those precious ones on the other side of the border was one of the toughest things I have ever had to do. I worked so hard to build trust, with the teens and pre-teens especially, only to end up saying good-bye far too quickly. As my two years in Mexico drew to a close, I asked God if I should stay a bit longer.

He replied, "No, you followed Me here, now follow Me home. It is time to write."

———

It's a bit difficult to explain what it felt like re-entering the States after two years, even though I had only been a few miles south of the border. After being immersed in an entirely different culture, it's quite tricky to return to a comfortable, "first-world" experience. though we had drug stores, grocery stores, and shopping malls on both sides of the border, and would cross into Texas fairly regularly, being back home was a world of difference. It seemed as though the process of re-entry was an ongoing experience. On par with leaving the children, it was one of the hardest things I've ever had to navigate. Some days were up while others were down, but the biggest takeaway for me has been learning to clearly communicate my needs and ask for (and give out) a surplus of grace and understanding.

At one point, I began to converse with other YWAM staff from my original DTS (the time in Wisconsin) about why the re-entry process was so difficult. One of them recommended and loaned me a book that I found to be very helpful. *Re-Entry: Making the Transition from Missions to Life at Home* by Peter Jordan began with practical tips to help one prepare to return home before ever leaving the field. From there, it branched off into several ways to process through various aspects of the transition, from connecting and communicating with those who financially and prayerfully supported you to dealing with issues of your heart and caring for your soul.

The mission field can be a lonely place. It was for me, at least. I think a big part of this was I moved to a city and culture I was only vaguely familiar with, a base I had never even visited before, without knowing a single person.

It took a while to transition in every way, but my favorite part was that I no longer had to check for cockroaches, spiders, or centipedes on all walls, floors, corners, and furniture in a room when entering before setting bags down! A con has been finding myself extremely overwhelmed and anxious in craft stores, frequently leaving in panic and tears.

Most people will only listen to missionaries recap their time on the field for so long before mentally checking out. I guess this is because they haven't had the same experiences; it can be difficult to relate, which is okay. I have so many stories that did not find their way onto these pages; perhaps some that will never be told to a broad audience at all.

There are often a great number of jokes made when somebody is headed to share the Gospel somewhere "nice" like Europe or the Caribbean—passive, jealous comments like, "Well, have fun 'suffering for the Gospel' on the beach! But hey, if the Lord really is calling you, go with Him!"

Clearly, people in those locations need to be told about Christ just as much as those in third world countries and even those back home; local outreach is just as important as abroad. Of course, there needs to be wisdom applied when going to these touristy types of places when it comes to dress codes, word choice (especially challenging if you are learning a new language in order to be there), and one's overall lifestyle. Since adoption is near to my heart, I'll add this too for perspective: adopting children locally is just as valid and crucial as adopting children from another country. Every child needs a good home; every person needs Jesus in their heart.

Many people openly question, "Why don't people just stay local for adoption and evangelism?" My own conclusion, formed through experience, is that we as Christians are supposed to simply love everybody. Believe it or not that includes foreigners, people in different lifestyles, and the homeless. Who will bring change to a child's life by offering to care for them, love them, and protect them?

I have heard stories of so many children who had no one to watch over them and ended up being snatched up by those with ill intentions and forced into lives of being prostituted (well, trafficked; there is no such thing as a "child prostitute"). Some traffickers and pimps even lurk near orphanages when the eighteenth birthdays of those inside draws near and they are turned loose into the real world, old enough to be on their own but too young to fend for themselves, preyed upon for their age and naivety. Often, without many life skills or any money, and no one to turn to besides their former caretakers who have greased palms from the lurkers and already moved on to the next batch of "unwanted" children.

The United States foster care system needs a lot of refining as well. I've come across many heartbreaking articles about reports of missing children who are found in trafficking rings cities or states away from where they should be. There are foster parents whom only want the extra government paycheck and don't care about the children at all. Some even rent the kids out to their neighbors and co-workers to perform sexual acts. This level of abuse is unacceptable, and it happens right in our backyards. I have faith that, one day, we will see the system redeemed!

Chapter 7

FAITH TRIP

uring the Spring of 2015, my good friend Marie and I both watched Darren Wilson's film *Holy Ghost*. If you're not familiar with the film, you really should see it. What happens is Darren and his crew decide to check out how the Holy Spirit is moving worldwide and document every step of their journey. It wasn't scripted, and began with them praying for direction and stepping out in faith. This process repeated itself throughout the film in different locations, and it was really cool to see how God showed up each time as they invited Him to act and many different ways. Their experiences were incredible and could not be invented or orchestrated by man apart from the guidance and work of the Holy Spirit. The ending, in particular, is especially moving.

As we discussed the film, Marie and I began to dream about how cool it would be to do something similar. Since we were both young, had seasonal jobs, and few commitments holding us down, we decided that this was a good plan. So, she came to Colorado to visit and we began to ask God what the time would become. We went in with our hearts and minds wide open to God's direction. For example, if we felt like He was leading us to go to a particular store and spend seven hours praying for strangers, we gladly would have. Even if we thought He said, *Go to the airport, I'm going to buy you both tickets through a stranger to somewhere for the wildest encounter either of you have ever seen!* we were open to Him doing the impossible. Although these particular scenarios never took place, God worked in other ways outside of what our minds could comprehend beforehand. It was truly a "faith trip" because our faith would expand as we stepped outside of our normal routines, not knowing what we would experience, where we would end up, or what the Lord would do in us and through us.

The first week we were together, we had many extended conversations, deep moments of connection, and special times with Jesus in worship and the Word. In addition, we consumed massive amounts of especially good coffee. A few days into the second week of her visit, we went for a little hike while we sought direction for what our next steps should be as far as the "trip." While we were waiting for God to speak, a man and woman came by and were looking out over the same view that we were. After a minute, they kissed, as if each were saying to the other, "I am even more entranced in you than I am by the beauty in front of us." In that moment, God spoke to my spirit and said, "You girls are more beautiful than this view, too."

As we continued to pray into our faith trip, Marie and I both strongly sensed that God was *not* directly leading us to go pray for people anywhere. Instead, we felt directed to bless people everywhere we went from the overflow we were receiving from God. Blessing comes from experiencing intimacy and hearing God's voice in the secret place of your heart. On this particular trip of faith, she and I spent time proverbially swimming and diving, all the while sinking deeper into our relationships with God and experiencing His delight in us. We listened to sermons on intimacy with the Lord, and little by little I felt Him gently beginning to heal my heart.

As Marie and I's friendship increased over those few weeks, I began to feel ready to officially report the incident from California where I was raped. Marie had volunteered at a rape crisis call center earlier that year, which perfectly positioned her to answer many of my questions about the reporting process, statute of limitations, and potential consequences. We approached the receptionist at a local dispatch center in Colorado and quickly learned that they could not receive the report as they did not have jurisdiction over where the incident occurred. Perhaps this has changed since then, hopefully, because I preferred to talk to someone about everything in person, but was told that we would either need to call it in or show up in the jurisdiction where the crime had occurred. After being told this, we walked back to my car where we called the correct authorities three states away. She held my hand as I retold each horrendous detail to a total stranger who we could not see, who was recording every word.

Some might wonder why I would report such an incident so long after it had taken place, and I'm happy to explain why.

First off, most rapes go unreported entirely, either because the victim is unaware that they should report what happened to them (me, until this point in time), or afraid of what might happen as a result of them doing so. While I now understand this, I think it's important to report incidents such as this in hopes that the person who committed the act will be brought to justice before they are able to harm anyone else.

Second, in my case, reporting the rape was a necessary component of my healing journey. It gave me peace, closure, and validated what I had been through. Once I got to a place where I was emotionally ready to report the crime and was able to do so, it was easier to begin to let it go and receive more of God's healing in greater measure.

A few days after reporting to the correct authorities, my information was passed along to a detective who called to confirm the details that had been recorded. This was great, even though he called three separate times to verify information. Though I appreciated their desire to be thorough and consistent and didn't mind too much, the wound had been re-opened and, in many ways, was still fresh. The detective emailed me a screenshot of my rapist's Facebook profile to ensure he had identified the correct person before he attempted to make contact with him in hopes of obtaining a confession.

I knew him to be an allusive party boy, and the chances of us extracting a confession out of him were slim to none. The detective continued to contact me in the weeks that followed, and we brainstormed ways of attempting to contact this guy in hopes that he would confess. The case came to a point where the biggest question I had to mull over was whether or not to seek prosecution, if indeed we were able to get him to confess.

I spent a great deal of time in prayer, and sought counsel from a few close friends and the pastors at my church. The next time I spoke with the detective, I asked him to shelve the case. We never contacted the man who raped me, for various reasons, and I am content with the incident having only been reported, even though prosecution was never pursued. I can rest in peace and trust that God will take care of the situation and bring about justice as He sees fit. He was there, He knows what happened, and He is able to fight for me in greater ways than I can fight for myself. It may seem like filing the report was a waste of time given this decision, but one key factor is if someone else reports a similar crime perpetrated by the same individual it will cause my report to resurface and I may be invited in to give a testimony. At this point, that is enough for me as I give this situation over to God.

That summer, Marie and I found peace, healing, and a deeper connection with the Lord. Through the "faith trip" moments, the Lord refreshed my soul and gave me the solace I so desperately needed. For that, I am forever grateful.

Chapter 8

GOD'S LEADING

*L*ate one night, during a time of worship at my adopted family's home, my "mom" approached me. She proceeded to thank me for sharing what God had put on my heart earlier that evening. She told me it can be hard for some to be bold and vulnerable with others by sharing what God has given them. Especially since there are some who cannot even grasp their minds around the reality that God desires a personal relationship with people and wants to speak to them. One of the ways He speaks is through Scripture, but there are also times when He chooses to speak straight to our hearts.

It can be upsetting when someone has a word from the Lord, even if it seems small or simple, but gets too fearful to share it out loud. I feel that when shyness wins, we all miss out on something God wants to say to us corporately, we can easily forget that He is personal. God could choose to tell each person in a group the same thing, but since each one of us are individuals, He speaks to us each differently. One way to think about it is that we, as the collective Church, are the body of Christ, as explained in Ephesians 4. We also "prophesy in part" (see 1 Corinthians chapters 12-14, chapter 13 in particular). We do not all get the same words, pictures, or songs because we have been given different gifts and been called to serve different functions in the Body of Christ. The way God communicates to me is probably different than how He might with you. I enjoy that He created us all in His image, while all so unique. As the Church, we are supposed to bring different aspects of God's character to the group in order to build one another up.

Sometimes, when God gives you a word to share, it can be intimidating. I was at the library one day when God began laying words on my heart for the girl using the computer next to me. I had never met her before, but I grabbed a pencil and a slip of paper and began writing her the following note of encouragement just as God spoke it. I then set it down on the desk next to her and walked away, praying the words resonated for her.

Just so you know, Jesus loves you
when it feels like your family and friends don't.
Your body, your heart, your mind, your soul—
He cares about it all, even when you stumble and fall.
In Him you are pure—cleaner than when
you were born, so don't let this world hit you
or try to cover you in scorn.

This may be the last thing you expected to hear today
or maybe just what you needed:
God is RAVISHED BY YOU so remember
that He is with you in all that you do.
See Psalm 37:4, Song of Solomon 4:9.

The more you step out and test your faith when the Holy Spirit nudges you, the more your faith will grow and expand into other areas of your life. Say "yes" to His prompting, even when it feels like He is challenging you. The more you do this, the more you will discover that God is faithful and you can always trust Him. He will never invite you to do something harmful. You will also begin to trust more in your ability to hear His voice in different situations. Trust in God is based in how you see Him. From experience, I've grown up seeing Him as my provider and my Heavenly Father. As your trust increases, your confidence will increase, and you'll be able to take greater risks to show a lost and hurting word the love of the Father.

After reading my story and what God has brought me through, I encourage you to step out as well. Go anywhere, ask God for something encouraging to say to anyone, and start a short conversation with them (about anything!), then ask how you can pray for them and do it immediately. Always be respectful of their time and preference. God will honor your courage to want to see people encounter Him, because He desperately wants that even more than we do.

I once heard the evangelist Todd White say something along the lines of, "You don't have to ask Holy Spirit *where* to go or *who* to pray for once you get there. He lives within you, which means that He is automatically wherever you are! If you aren't sure who to pray for, find one person who Jesus did not die for, then pray for anyone else."

Something else I heard Todd say is, "Other people's lives depend on me walking out what Love looks like every day."

Simply remember, though, that people are not projects.

I love sharing my story, the one spread over these pages, because God said this book will demonstrate His faithfulness and bring hope to readers who are dealing with similar things that He has already seen me through. What He says does not return void; we can stand on His promises (Isaiah 55:11, 2 Corinthians 1:20). Most of all, I love admiring God's hand in everyday life. Being in coffee shops and other busy places, you can see this while observing your surroundings. One day, while I was out writing, I involuntarily smiled every time someone came in through the door over four hours because I could see how beautiful and diverse we are, yet we are all created in God's image (Genesis 1:27). Most of the people who entered the coffee shop noticed my smile and smiled back. I hope they felt welcomed and a sense of belonging, and hopefully they saw Jesus in my eyes. He changes everything.

AFTERWORD

*a*fter reading my story, there is a question that nearly always pops up: *Why do bad things happen to good people, even ones who love and live for the Lord?* Believing that God only gives good things, I could not fathom anything I did as a little kid to "deserve" to lose my dad. Later, I did not understand why I was repeatedly singled out and yelled at frequently, or why I have had to battle depression off and on for half of my life. Nobody deserves to be raped. I did not do anything to invite these things or to cause them.

In one of our conversations, Marie said, "I find it comforting to be reminded that we live in a broken world and we, as broken people, have free will, which is sometimes used to create more brokenness. But, God can, will, and *wants* to redeem those broken things. He can use them, in His infinite wisdom, to bring about good things in our lives. It's hard to define the difference between God *causing* something to happen and *allowing* something to happen. Regardless of which it is, I know He uses evil things for our ultimate good."

As we acknowledge God as our Creator and Savior, we must also acknowledge satan as a liar and destroyer (John 10:10). Honestly, if not for the grace and plan of God, I do not think I would be alive to write this book. You have read about how I repeatedly went to bed with serrated kitchen knives in high school but somehow managed to wake up unharmed. Through it all, I'm still breathing. I'm still here. I do still struggle with the residual effects and PTSD from the sexual assault, as well as from the verbal abuse, yelling, and door slamming. However, let it be known that the traumatic events do not *define* me whatsoever. As they surface, I actively invite God to heal me from them while taking practical steps to mitigate the effects. Of course, some days are better than others, and that is okay.

Something I've noted while healing from situations, specifically with a narcissist and a rapist, is how I relate to men in and out of the Church. Although neither abuser truly lived as one while we knew each other, they claimed to be Christians before, while, and after abusing me. I always try to see the best in people and end up either overextending trust or I keep my distance altogether. When I'm in a situation where I find myself outnumbered by men, regardless of whether I'm at a night of worship or in the aisle of a bookstore, my entire body tenses up and I become very anxious while lining up all visible exit routes, from closest to farthest away.

Another prevalent effect of PTSD that I currently see in myself is the inability to consistently and naturally convert short-term memories into long-term memories. For example, while I'm at work, I need to take copious notes of instruction and read them back if there is time. If I don't, I will completely forget the tasks that were required of me. Others might have to write things down at work too, but for me, I normally need to write every detail down, otherwise, it is as though I never heard it. Similarly, when making plans verbally for any type of meeting or outing with friends or family, if it is solely spoken but not written down in a text or on paper, I'll most likely forget it. This trait, I have noticed, is especially irritating to friends who value being listened to and validated. I also value being heard and understood, and go into conversations and try so hard to do these things as a way to honor them, but often catch my mind in a totally different place. For so long I thought it was due to a lack of intentionality and listening skills on my part. In diving into research on the topic of trauma induced memory loss, I've realized that it is so much more than that, and I appreciate that much research has been completed on this topic. Taking the time to ask the questions and do the research, not only validates what I'm going through, it also helps me realize that I'm not alone in this experience.

I've come to realize that there is a name for this—*dissociation*. While it can be difficult to recognize that one has been dissociated, it's actually a natural reaction to trauma, a numbing of sorts, where the brain says "Nope, can't do this right now." I used to immediately feel discouraged when I would catch myself mentally stepping away from what is happening right in front of me, but I'm coming to a place of learning to be patient with myself and feel rough feelings so they can process themselves and move on.

Writing this book has been an honor for me, and I hope somehow it will be helpful to you in your life and struggles. If so, please share your copy with a friend or leave it on public transit or anywhere for someone else to stumble across and feel less alone.

I'd leave you with these truths:

One, to know how important you are. Your life was given to you for a reason because you have a destiny.

Two, nothing you have done before this moment is unforgivable; God's love is still far greater.

And finally, there is purpose behind every breath you take in and send out of your beautiful body. I encourage you to seek God for that specific purpose for your life. If you *think* you may know, confirm it. Spend time listening to God for yourself. Once you know your identity and destiny, your circumstances will probably no longer seem *as* overwhelming.

You can face a challenge, breathe deep, and say: I am loved. There is hope. I have help. In my weakness, He is strong.

Stay strong,

Love in Christ,

Ellie

Therefore in Christ Jesus I have found reason for boasting in things pertaining to God. For I will not presume to speak of anything except what Christ has accomplished through me, resulting in the obedience of the Gentiles by word and deed, in the power of signs and wonders, in the power of the Spirit; so that from Jerusalem and round about as far as Illyricum I have fully preached the Gospel of Christ.

—Romans 15:17-19

ADDITIONAL RESOURCES

Resources for Readers (mostly specific to the United States):
NOTE: This list is not extensive. Hopefully it is encouraging,
however, to find help and healing for you or a friend's struggles. Advocates and responders on these text lines are trained
and can help you find counseling or therapy options in your
area if you are interested or are unable to procure for yourself
for any reason.

**Addiction, Depression, Suicide Prevention, Self-
Injury, Trauma, and more:**

> To Write Love On Her Arms: twloha.com/find-help/
> (resources listed for multiple countries)

> National Suicide Prevention Hotline:
> 1 (800) 273-TALK(8255)

> Substance Abuse & Mental Health Services:
> 1 (800) 662-HELP(4357)

> Hope for the Day: hftd.org

**For more information on the ties between the pornography
industry and human trafficking, the effects of consumption,
etc. from page 44:**

> fightthenewdrug.org

How to learn about, recognize, and report suspected human trafficking in your area:

Learn about it at polarisproject.org and exoduscry.com

Human Trafficking Hotline—(888) 373-7888 or text "HELP" to BeFree (233733); call or text for help or to share tips with authorities

Sexual Crimes Against You or a Loved One

National Sexual Assault Hotline—
(800) 656-HOPE (4673)
rainn.org for info and live chat option

rainn.org/effects-sexual-violence

rainn.org/articles/warning-signs-young-children

RAINN offers the following free services: confidential support from trained staff, support finding local health facilities that has trained staff to help survivors of sexual assault and offers services including sexual assault forensic exams ("rape kits", etc.), someone to help you talk through what happened, local resources that can assist with your next step towards healing and recovery, referrals for long term support in your area, information about the laws in your community, & basic information about medical concerns.

The Blue Bench—303-322-7273
(Specific to Colorado)
Toll Free 1-888-394-8044

thebluebench.org
Solid group, recommended by many First Responders who have worked together with the group.

**More info on these two numbers (RAINN & Blue Bench): IF you or someone you know is sexually assaulted, get the victim to the police station closest to where the assault happened AS SOON AS POSSIBLE after leaving the scene. *Not everyone is taught this because it is altogether uncomfortable, but it is imperative to justice pulling through (collecting testimony + evidence while all as raw and fresh as possible). Do not shower or brush your teeth before going to police. If you change clothes, turn in unwashed articles of all available clothing, bedding, etc. from the crime scene in a paper bag (so they "breathe"). These may be returned to you after tests are run for DNA samples if you ask the officer who you hand it to make a note you'd like to save them if at all possible. Police or a Victim Advocate will offer you Victim's Rights Resources for follow up before you leave. It is recommended but not required to bring a friend with you for emotional support.